Cambridge Elements ≡

Elements in the History of Constantinople
edited by
Peter Frankopan
University of Oxford

THE HIPPODROME OF CONSTANTINOPLE

Engin Akyürek
Koç University

CAMBRIDGE
UNIVERSITY PRESS

CAMBRIDGE
UNIVERSITY PRESS

University Printing House, Cambridge CB2 8BS, United Kingdom

One Liberty Plaza, 20th Floor, New York, NY 10006, USA

477 Williamstown Road, Port Melbourne, VIC 3207, Australia

314–321, 3rd Floor, Plot 3, Splendor Forum, Jasola District Centre,
New Delhi – 110025, India

103 Penang Road, #05–06/07, Visioncrest Commercial, Singapore 238467

Cambridge University Press is part of the University of Cambridge.

It furthers the University's mission by disseminating knowledge in the pursuit of
education, learning, and research at the highest international levels of excellence.

www.cambridge.org
Information on this title: www.cambridge.org/9781108931984
DOI: 10.1017/9781108942959

© Engin Akyürek 2021

First published 2021

A catalogue record for this publication is available from the British Library.

ISBN 978-1-108-93198-4 Paperback
ISSN 2514-3891 (online)
ISSN 2514-3883 (print)

The Hippodrome of Constantinople

Elements in the History of Constantinople

DOI: 10.1017/9781108942959
First published online: September 2021

Engin Akyürek
Koç University
Author for correspondence: Engin Akyürek, engin.akyurek@gmail.com

Abstract: The Hippodrome of Constantinople was constructed in the fourth century AD, by the Roman Emperor Constantine I, in his new capital. Throughout Byzantine history, the Hippodrome served as a ceremonial, sportive, and recreational centre of the city; in the early period, it was used mainly as an arena for very popular, competitive, and occasionally violent chariot races, while the Middle Ages witnessed the imperial ceremonies coming to the fore gradually, although the races continued. The ceremonial and recreational role of the Hippodrome somehow continued during the Ottoman period. Being the oldest structure in the city, the Hippodrome has witnessed exciting chariot races, ceremonies glorifying victorious emperors as well as the charioteers, and the riots that shook the imperial authority. Today, looking to the remnants of the Hippodrome, one can imagine the glorious past of the site.

Keywords: Byzantium/Byzantine, ceremonies, chariot, Constantinople, Hippodrome

ISBNs: 9781108931984 (PB), 9781108942959 (OC)
ISSNs: 2514-3891 (online), 2514-3883 (print)

Contents

1 Introduction

The word hippodrome, which derives from the Greek *hippos* (horse) and *drómos* (course, running way), refers to a venue where horse races are held.[1] Today, the word hippodrome is used in many languages to denote a location dedicated to horse races. In the ancient Greek world, horse and chariot races were part of sports competitions organised for various occasions. It was not professional teams but individual athletes who competed in these races. In Homer's epic *Iliad*, one of the earliest recorded horse races was held to honour the funeral of Patroclus. Although the epic dates from very early times, it refers to elements of chariot races which would continue to develop later in the Greek and Roman world: the drawing of lots to determine starting positions, a long track with a turning post at the end, and chariots that ran counter-clockwise.

The first structures – or more accurately the first racing areas – that could be called hippodromes emerged in ancient Greece, and following a long process of evolution, they found their ideal form in Roman civilisation. In Greece, the first hippodromes were generally arranged in a rather simple fashion. There was a long and wide flat where chariots would tour and race. Around or beside this was a zone dedicated to spectators, and there was a setup that allowed the chariots to start the race simultaneously. The oldest known ancient hippodrome is the Olympia hippodrome in Greece mentioned by the Greek traveller and geographer Pausanias (*c.*110–80 CE). The hippodrome, which no longer exists, was a wide, flat open area about 600 metres long. The competition area featured starting gates, ensuring that competitors began the race at the same time. There was also a barrier with a return point at the end, which would divide the wide area from the middle into two racetracks, as well as a finishing line. In addition, there was a low hill on the north side of the track, and an artificial bank on the southern side, to make it possible for spectators to watch the races more comfortably.[2] This area, which is assumed to be on the south side of the stadium in Olympia, was completely washed away by the Alpheios River over time, hence no archaeological data have survived to indicate what kind of a structure it was.

In the world of Rome, the hippodrome developed into a typical Roman institution, with its special architecture that could accommodate most citizens of the city, and with its new functions along with chariot races.[3] When the tradition of horse chariot races was brought to Rome, hippodromes took on additional social and political functions. These races, featuring chariots known

---

[1] Henry George Liddell et al., *A Greek and English Lexicon* (Oxford: Clarendon Press, 1940).
[2] John H. Humphrey, *Roman Circuses: Arenas for Chariot Racing* (London: Batsford, 1986), 7–9.
[3] Ibid., for Roman period hippodromes.

as *quadriga* drawn by four horses, became much more than sports competitions, and turned into entertainment events for masses of spectators organised by professional teams. Eventually they also became part of the imperial ceremonies. In compliance with their new functions, hippodromes emerged as a structure type with specific standards. The race area, reaching 500 metres in length, was split with a barrier in the middle into two tracks, return signs were positioned at either end of this barrier, gates that opened simultaneously were placed at the starting point, and two- or three-floor bleachers surrounding the racetrack from three sides were built to accommodate a huge number of spectators. In Rome, the most prominent example of this new hippodrome architecture is the Circus Maximus. To satisfy the people of Rome, this immense structure was built in 46 BCE by Emperor Julius Caesar (100–44 BCE) on the site of a previous hippodrome from an earlier age. The hippodrome, which featured wooden benches at first, was built permanently in stone during the era of Emperor Trajan (r. 98–117 CE). The course of the Circus Maximus was 550 metres long by 80 metres wide and was divided in two by a barrier called a spina wall, and on this were two obelisks, brought from Egypt, and various statues. On either end of the spina, there were conical turning posts. Dolphin-shaped lap markers would be turned to indicate each lap completed on the track. Race chariots would emerge onto the track through the twelve gates that started the race by opening simultaneously. The Circus Maximus, which could accommodate more than 100,000 spectators, became the new entertainment and ceremony venue of the city of Rome, and gained great popularity among the people. The final chariot race in the Circus Maximus was held in 549 by the Ostrogothic king Totila (r. 541–52 CE), who ruled over Rome at that time. Later, the structure was left to its own devices. The Circus Maximus, which inspired all hippodromes in the empire, became a model for hippodromes later built in many prominent Roman cities. Although the Circus Maximus can be perceived in all its glory in the context of the modern city of Rome, the example that best illustrates the details of the architectural elements of a Roman hippodrome is the Leptis Magna hippodrome near Khoms, Libya, which is in a much better state of preservation. It has survived to the present day with its rows of stone seats, its spina dividing the racetrack, and other architectural details largely intact.[4]

Hippodromes, where various shows and ceremonies such as chariot races, gladiator fights, wild animal fights, pantomimes, and dances were organised, were among the most important public spaces of a Roman city, and one of the most prominent elements of Roman urban design. Roman hippodromes were

---

[4] Ibid., 25–40.

much more than an arena or venue for chariot races, other sports activities, or entertainment; they also became a show of imperial power, and a symbol of the imperial ceremonies and cult, as well as a setting where important proclamations of the emperor were made, where victories were celebrated, and a political and social space where the city population gathered.[5]

The sixth-century Byzantine historian John Malalas (*c*.490–570s) claims that the first hippodrome in Rome was built by the founder of the city, Romulus. There is no data concerning which hippodrome this is and whether its ruins are still visible. Beyond doubt, the claim written by Malalas centuries after the Romulus legend has no historical validity; however, what he wrote about the rationale for Romulus establishing the hippodrome and the importance of hippodrome symbolism remains valid for his era. According to Malalas, '[Romulus] built the hippodrome in Rome, wishing to direct the mass of the people of Rome because they were rioting and attacking him'.[6] In Rome, during the Festival of the Sun, the first chariot races were again organised by Romulus 'in honour of the four elements subordinate to it [the Sun], that is earth, sea, fire and air'.[7] Of the two chariots, the blue one raced on behalf of Poseidon, while the green one raced on behalf of Demeter.

Malalas also states that the symbolism associated with a Roman hippodrome is as significant as its architectural forms, and that both were carried over to Byzantine-era hippodromes, especially to the one in Constantinople, also known as 'New Rome'. According to Malalas, the structure of the hippodrome was modelled on the regulation of the world, in other words, the sky, the earth, and the seas. The twelve-section starting gate was related to the twelve houses of the zodiac cycle, the racing track symbolised the earth, while the spina represented the sea surrounded by land. Malalas indicates that, of the four chariots that participated in the first race ever organised by Romulus in Rome, the green one symbolised the earth, the blue symbolised the sea, the red symbolised the fire, while the white one symbolised the air.[8]

For a city, the hippodrome was also the proof of 'Roman' identity, and an instrument of 'Romanisation'.[9] In the second and third centuries, the Roman

[5] Cyril Mango, Alexander Kazhdan, and Anthony Cutler, 'Hippodromes', in *The Oxford Dictionary of Byzantium*, ed. Alexander Kazhdan et al. (New York and Oxford: Oxford University Press, 1991), 934–6.

[6] *The Chronicle of John Malalas*. Translated by Elizabeth Jeffreys, Michael Jeffreys, and Roger Scott (Melbourne: Australian Association for Byzantine Studies, 1986), 92 (book 7, 173).

[7] Ibid., 92 (book 7, 174).   [8] Ibid., 93 (book 7, 175).

[9] Gilbert Dagron, 'Bir Roma'dan Diğerine/From One Rome to the Other', in *Hippodrom/ Atmeydanı: İstanbul'un Tarih Sahnesi/Hippodrome/Atmeydanı: A Stage for Istanbul's History*, vol. 1, ed. Brigitte Pitarakis (Istanbul: Pera Müzesi Yayınları, 2010), 31.

hippodrome underwent a few negligible changes but spread to all important cities of the empire along with its symbolic elements. Because the lands of the Roman Empire spanned such a wide area, the emperors frequently took up long-term residence in cities outside of Rome. As a token of imperial presence in these cities, they built hippodromes and organised chariot races.[10] Hence, it was emphasised that the emperor was in that city, and that the city was a prominent part of the Roman Empire. Hippodromes existed in the eastern provinces of the Roman Empire, especially in cities such as Alexandria, Antioch, Berytos, Nicomedia, Thessaloniki, and Tyre where imperial residences were also located.[11] Almost all of these were built in the third century, starting from the era of Septimius Severus (r. 193–211). During this time, imperial residences increased in number and spread to various eastern cities, a phenomenon which continued during the era of the Tetrarchs (293–305).

The hippodromes of the Roman period were generally constructed outside the city walls. This was of course because it was quite difficult to find an area of this magnitude within the walls of the city; however, in the period of the Tetrarchs and later, starting in the era of Emperor Constantine I (r. 324–37), hippodromes were built inside city walls, generally attached to the imperial palace as an integral part of palace buildings.[12] In Constantinople, the imperial palace and the hippodrome built by Constantine I were attached to each other, and a direct passage connected the palace to the imperial box inside the hippodrome.[13] Hippodromes, which were in a sense built as symbols of imperial power, were not considered separate from the imperial residence. Although many of these have vanished without leaving any archaeologic traces, it is likely that just like the one in Constantinople, these hippodromes were built attached to the imperial palace or in its vicinity.[14]

2 History of the Hippodrome

The Hippodrome of Constantinople was modelled on its prototype, the Circus Maximus in Rome. The hippodrome was built in the centre of the city of Constantinople, in a prominent position on the eastern end of the historical peninsula known today as Sultanahmet (Figure 1). This area, which constituted the core of Byzantine public life, featured three significant building complexes:

---

[10] Ibid.
[11] Gilbert Dagron, *L'hippodrome de Constantinople: Jeux, peuple et politique.* Bibliothèque des Histoires (Paris: Éditions Gallimard, 2011), 33; for a list, see Alan Cameron, *Circus Factions, Blues and Greens at Rome and Byzantium* (Oxford: Clarendon Press, 1976), 208–9.
[12] Mango, Kazhdan, and Cutler, 'Hippodromes', 935.
[13] *Chronicle of Malalas,* 174 (book 13, 7).
[14] Cyril Mango, 'Konstantinopolis Hippodromu'nun Tarihçesi/A History of the Hippodrome of Constantinople', in *Hippodrom/Atmeydanı*, vol. 1, 37.

Figure 1 Aerial view of the Hippodrome, Gabam Archives, photo by G. Tan

Saint Sophia, the cathedral church of Constantinople and the adjacent patriarchal palace; the imperial palace and the Senate building; and the Hippodrome. On its eastern side, the Hippodrome was adjacent to the Great Palace (*Palatium Magnum*). To its north-east was the Zeuxippus, the most important baths of the city, while to its north was Mese, the main avenue of the city, and the Million Stone, the monument that represented the starting point (point zero) of all imperial roads. The Augusteion Square to its north-east was located between the city's cathedral, the Senate building, the imperial palace, and the Hippodrome. Due to this position, the Hippodrome and its vicinity made up the most valuable section of the city, its centre. For many important personalities, having a private palace in the vicinity of the Hippodrome was a status symbol. Hence, on the north-east side of the Hippodrome, the ruins of the palaces of two important fifth-century state officials, Antiochus and Lausos, have survived. Antiochus, who was of Persian origin, was the highest-ranking eunuch (*praepositus sacri cubiculi*) in the palace of Theodosius II (r. 408–50), and he had his palace built right next to the Hippodrome. In 439, while Antiochus was still alive, the emperor confiscated this palace, and had the round, domed reception hall (*triclinium*) transformed into a church. The structure known today as the Church of Saint Euphemia is the reception hall of this palace.[15] The palace of Lausos was to the north of this, and its round plan *triclinium* and the lower walls of the parts extending west are still visible today.

Who constructed the Hippodrome, Septimius Severus or Constantine I? This issue, which is ambiguous in Byzantine sources, is also a subject of discussion in the modern literature.[16] Some Byzantine sources state that the construction of the Hippodrome of Constantinople was first started by the Romans at the end of the second century. Emperor Septimius Severus organised a campaign against Pescennius Niger, the governor of Syria who was claiming the imperial throne, and in 196, following a two-year siege, Emperor Septimius Severus took Byzantium, and started the reconstruction of the ruined city, as well as the construction of the Hippodrome. In the *Patria*, a tenth-century collection of texts devoted to the history and the monuments of Constantinople, it is stated that the Hippodrome was built by Severus on gardens belonging to two brothers and a widow.[17] Although there is no information on whether the structure was completed or whether it entered service, the *Patria* states that Severus completed one side of the bleachers, but then had to head for Rome upon receiving news that it was being besieged by the Gauls, and the bleachers on the other side were left incomplete.[18] It was Constantine who constructed the other side of the bleachers, the two galleries, the top part of the starting gates, the semi-circular south end called the sphendone, and the benches allocated to the circus factions; he collected important sculptures from many cities and temples of the empire and placed them in the Hippodrome. Among these were twenty sculptures, including the statue of Augustus brought from Rome, and the statue of Emperor Diocletian (r. 284–305) brought from Nicomedia (modern-day Izmit).[19] However, although we find a lot of information about the Hippodrome in the *Patria*, these texts should not be taken as true 'historical documents' per se; the

---

[15] For the Palace of Antiochos and Church of Saint Euphemia, see Rudolf Naumann and Hans Belting, *Die Euphemia-Kirche am Hippodrom zu Istanbul und ihre Fresken, Istanbuler Forschungen Band 25* (Berlin: Verlag Gebr. Mann, 1966).

[16] See Dagron, *L'hippodrome de Constantinople*, 37–42.

[17] *Accounts of Medieval Constantinople, The Patria*, translated by Albrecht Berger (London and Cambridge, MA: Harvard University Press, 2013), 25 (I, 40).

[18] Ibid., 37 (I, 61–2).   [19] Ibid., 99–100 (II, 73).

folkloric side of these texts, full of legends and myths,[20] should be taken into account.

The *Chronicon Paschale,* another Byzantine-era source, repeats the same information:

> 'he [Constantine] also completed the Hippodrome, adorning it with works in
> bronze and with every excellence, and made in it a box for imperial viewing in
> likeness of the one which is in Rome. And made a great palace near the same
> Hippodrome, and the ascent from the palace to the box in the Hippodrome by
> way of the kochlias, as it is called.'[21]

The same information also appears in Malalas' chronicle.[22] This information from Byzantine sources is widely accepted by many scholars today. According to this, when Emperor Constantine I declared the city of Byzantium the new capital of the Roman Empire in 330 CE and initiated a comprehensive construction effort, he either completed or expanded the Hippodrome of Severus. Cyril Mango, however, does not agree with the view that the first construction of the Hippodrome of Constantinople coincides with the era of Septimius Severus, and instead he attributes it to Constantine.[23] Indeed, if the construction of the Hippodrome was started in 196 by Severus, it does not seem logical that it would only be completed by Constantine I 134 years later in 330. Besides, the fact that no archaeological data that can be dated to the Severan era have been found supports Mango's claim. It is more plausible that Constantine had the Hippodrome built in the fourth century. As Constantinople, the new imperial capital bearing the founder's name, was being built, the imperial palace and the adjacent Hippodrome were its first and most important structures. Two explanations can be provided for why some Byzantine records attribute the first building of the Hippodrome to Septimius Severus – either the structure of the Hippodrome commissioned by Severus was too small and simple, and it was rebuilt in a size befitting the new role of the city reconstructed as the new capital of the Roman Empire, or the aim was to prove that the construction date was much earlier as a result of the effort to associate the new capital of the empire with Rome.

The fact that the Hippodrome was built by Constantine I, and that prominent monuments from all over the empire were brought there is no doubt connected

---

[20] Dagron, *L'hippodrome de Constantinople,* 23–4.

[21] *Chronicon Paschale, 284–628 A.D.,* translated by Michael Whitby and Mary Whitby (Liverpool: Liverpool University Press, 2007), 16 (328).

[22] *Chronicle of Malalas,* 174 (book 13, 7–8).

[23] Mango, 'History of the Hippodrome', 38–9; Jonathan Bardill, 'Konstantinopolis Hippodromu'nun Mimarisi ve Arkeolojisi/The Architecture and Archaeology of the Hippodrome in Constantinople', in *Hippodrom/Atmeydanı,* vol. 1, 94.

with the emperor's declaration of the city as the new capital of the Roman Empire. Constantinople is the 'New Rome', so its hippodrome should be of a magnificence to match the Circus Maximus in Rome. Hence, 'New Rome' was elevated up to the status of 'Old Rome'. On the other hand, the fact that Constantine had his imperial palace built adjacent to the existing hippodrome shows its connection with the cult of the emperor. The imperial box, which was built on the east bleachers of the Hippodrome, had been designed as a direct extension of the palace into the Hippodrome itself.

The Hippodrome of Constantinople has certainly been a key component of the city and has always played a major role throughout its history. They shared the same historical destiny and lived victories and catastrophes together through thick and thin. In particular, the frequent fires and earthquakes that impacted the city and the insurrections that typically started from the Hippodrome and spread to the city caused damage to the Hippodrome in places; however, things were patched up, and the Hippodrome continued to serve its citizens and its emperor. Some of the critical moments of this common destiny have survived to the present day. In 406, a fire devastated most of the city and damaged the entrance section of the Hippodrome as well as some benches. In 407, repairs were undertaken by Emperor Arcadius (r. 395–408) and stairs going to the portico were built.[24] Throughout its history, the Hippodrome witnessed many insurrections and riots. The first major insurrection occurred in 445, at the end of the reign of Emperor Theodosius II, but most of the others coincided with the era of Emperor Anastasius I (r. 491–518). Insurrections of various sizes started in the Hippodrome in 493, 498, 499, 501, 507, 514, and 520. During these, the Hippodrome was subjected to some damage, especially to the wooden benches, which were burnt.

However, the Nika Revolt, which broke out in the sixth century during the era of Emperor Justinian (r. 527–65), had serious implications for the history of the Hippodrome as well as that of the city, to which it caused serious damage. In January 532, the protest that the Green and Blue factions started in the Hippodrome eventually turned into the largest insurgence in the history of Constantinople. Because the insurgents were screaming out 'victory' (*nika*), this event came to be known as the Nika Revolt.[25] Justinian and his wife Theodora were supporting the Blues among the circus factions, and this caused great discontent among the Greens. As the unrest continued in the

---

[24] *Chronicon Paschale*, 60–1 (406–7).
[25] The Nika Revolt was detailed in Byzantine sources. See *Chronicle of Malalas*, 275–81 (book 18, 71); *Chronicon Paschale*, 114–27 (531); Procopius, *The Secret History: With Related Texts*, translated and edited with an introduction by Anthony Kaldellis (Indianapolis: Hackett Publishing, 2010), 136–44.

city streets, one person from each of the Blue and Green factions was arrested and condemned to death, which escalated the situation, and caused the two rival teams to unite. On 13 January, during the chariot races organised in the Hippodrome, the Green and Blue supporters saw Emperor Justinian and Empress Theodora in the imperial box across from the bleachers allocated to circus factions, and they demanded the pardon of the two arrested supporters and the removal of the head of the central administration (*praetorian prefect*), John the Cappadocian. The emperor complied with these requests, but this still did not satisfy the insurgents. In the evening, the events grew and went beyond the Hippodrome, and the angry mobs attacked the *praetorium*, the centre of the city prefecture. During these events, the crowd gathered in the Augusteion Square in front of the Saint Sophia Church. The anger of the insurgents was directed towards the imperial palace, the official emperor statues, the patriarchate, and the patriarchal images, and these were vandalised as they were seen as the symbols of authority.[26] Thus, the main entrance (Chalke Gate) of the imperial palace located at the eastern edge of the Augusteion Square, the Senate building next to it, the patriarchal palace and Saint Sophia, some residences belonging to the wealthy, the Zeuxippus baths, and the *porticos* in the area all the way to the Forum of Constantine (present-day Çemberlitaş), which were the authority symbols of the city, were burnt and destroyed. The historian Procopius (*c*.500–70), who witnessed the period, states that the city was damaged as if it had been seized and set ablaze by an enemy.[27] The rebels brought Hypatios, the nephew of Anastasius, into the imperial box in the Hippodrome and declared him emperor. While Justinian was making plans to put his gold on a boat and to go by sea to take refuge in Herakleia (modern-day Marmara Ereğlisi), the Empress Theodora persuaded him to stay in the city and fight. One of his faithful generals Belisarius went into the imperial box, arrested Hypatios along with his brother Pompeios and brought them to face Justinian. The next day, both were executed. Belisarius and the commander in chief of the armies (*magister militum*), Mundus, who happened to be in the city at that moment with 1,500 troops, entered the Hippodrome and, according to Procopius, killed about 30,000 to quell the uprising. After this event, chariot races and shows in the Hippodrome were discontinued for a few years. This revolt, which is one of the most important events in the history of Constantinople and the Hippodrome, was widely covered by Procopius, as well as the prominent Byzantine historiographer Theophanes (the Confessor,

---

[26] Averil Cameron, *The Mediterranean World in Late Antiquity, A.D. 395–400* (London and New York: Routledge, 1993), 172.

[27] Procopius, *Secret History*, 138 (8–9).

*c.*760–817).[28] The wooden benches that were burnt and damaged during this insurgence were later replaced with stone benches by Emperor Justinian. As Hippodrome races and circus factions were increasingly integrated into the imperial ceremonies, the number of insurgences instigated by these parties diminished.

Hippodromes witnessed uprisings against imperial authority not only in the capital Constantinople but in other cities of the empire as well. In 390, while Emperor Theodosius I (r. 378–95) was in Thessaloniki, during the races in the hippodrome, spectators in the bleachers insulted him and a revolt started, during which the archers of Theodosius killed 15,000 – exaggerated for sure – people in the hippodrome.[29] Malalas reports an insurgence, from 494 to 495, that Greens and Blues instigated together in Antioch during the reign of Emperor Anastasius.[30]

Chariot races were held quite frequently during the late Roman–early Byzantine period, but during the seventh and eighth centuries, interest declined all over the empire. During this period, almost all hippodromes in country towns were abandoned, and only the Hippodrome of Constantinople at the centre of the empire continued to exist. Yet, even here the races were no longer the competitive and occasionally violent sport of the late antique era, and turned into grandiose pageants. Except for the scheduled races that were repeated every year, such as those celebrating the foundation of the city, the chariot races were held less frequently, about three to four times a year, on the occasion of an accession to the throne, the birth of a prince, the marriage of the emperor, a celebration of victory, or the welcoming of foreign ambassadors and important guests.[31] This period of the city's history, which many historians call 'the dark age', witnessed major catastrophes such as earthquakes and plague epidemics,[32] and it was quite uninspiring both for life in the capital city and for the Hippodrome.

Much of our knowledge about the use of the Hippodrome in the Middle Ages comes from the tenth-century text *The Book of Ceremonies* by Emperor

---

[28] Ibid., 144 (2.54–6); *The Chronicle of Theophanes Confessor: Byzantine and Near Eastern History AD 284–813*, translated with introduction and commentary by Cyril Mango and Roger Scott (Oxford: Clarendon Press, 1997), 276–80 (182–6). Modern literature also repeats this information: James Allan Evans, *The Emperor Justinian and the Byzantine Empire*. Greenwood Guides to Historic Events of the Ancient World (Westport, CT and London: Greenwood Press, 2005), 15–20.

[29] *Chronicle of Malalas*, 188 (book 13, 43).   [30] Ibid., 220 (book 16, 2).

[31] Mango, 'History of the Hippodrome', 40–1.

[32] The siege of Constantinople by Persian (610), Avar (619 and 626), and Arab (starting in 674 and 714) armies; the earthquake that caused great destruction in the city in 740; and the plague epidemic that killed a considerable part of the city's population in 747 are several of these calamities.

Constantine VII Porphyrogennetos (r. 913–59).[33] In this text, the organisation of the chariot races and the imperial ceremonies held in the Hippodrome are described in detail. Although chariot races were still held, in the tenth and probably eleventh centuries, the Hippodrome was mainly a venue for the imperial ceremonies.

From the accounts of the Spanish-Jewish traveller Benjamin of Tudela (1130–73), who visited Constantinople during the reign of Emperor Manuel Komnenos (r. 1143–80), we know that under the Komnenian dynasty, in parallel to the revival experienced in the empire at large, a revival was also seen in the capital, and entertainment resumed in the Hippodrome. Although Benjamin does not specifically mention chariot races in his travelogue, he does talk about various types of entertainment, including fights with wild animals:

> Close to the walls of the palace is also a place of amusement belonging to the king, which is called the Hippodrome, and every year on the anniversary of the birth of Jesus the king gives a great entertainment there. And in that place men from all the races of the world come before the king and queen with jugglery and without jugglery, and they introduce lions, leopards, bears, and wild asses, and they engage them in combat with one another; and the same thing is done with the birds. No entertainment like this is to be found in any other land.[34]

The final recorded chariot race was held during the era of Alexios III Angelos (r. 1195–203), in 1200.[35] The fire of 1203 greatly damaged the Hippodrome, especially the western wing. After this event, the Hippodrome was not repaired again; a year later, the city was seized by the armies of the Fourth Crusade, and the Byzantine Empire had to continue its existence in exile for some time.

The coup de grâce to the Hippodrome was inflicted by the armies of the Fourth Crusade who seized Constantinople and established a Latin kingdom from 1204 to 1261. In this period, like other important buildings of the city, the Hippodrome was plundered and ruined. Sculptures were either smashed or smuggled to Europe, bronze statues were melted and used for minting coins and producing weapons. Four life-size bronze horse sculptures, located on the entrance gate of the Hippodrome, were removed and taken to Venice, where they were placed onto the entrance of the Basilica of San Marco on the command of Enrico Dandolo.[36]

---

[33] Constantine Porphyrogennetos, *The Book of Ceremonies*, two vols, translated by Anne Moffatt and Maxeme Tall (Canberra: Australian Association for Byzantine Studies, 2012).

[34] *The Itinerary of Benjamin of Tudela,* critical text, translation, and commentary by Marcus Nathan Adler (London: Oxford University Press, 1907), 12–13 (21).

[35] Mango, 'History of the Hippodrome', 42.

[36] Doge of Venice (1192–205). He was an important figure in the Fourth Crusade army that was occupying Constantinople.

The historian Niketas Khoniates (*c*.1155–220), who witnessed the era, relates what the Latin army did to the sculptures in the city, and states that one of the prominent bronze statues of the Hippodrome depicting Herakles was melted down for minting coins:

> These barbarians, haters of the beautiful, did not allow the statues standing in the Hippodrome and other marvellous works of art to escape destruction, but all were made into coins. Thus great things were exchanged for small ones, those works fashioned at hugh expense were converted into worthless copper coins.[37]

In 1261, after the Byzantines took the city back from the Latins, the Hippodrome was no longer fit to fulfil its former function. During the last centuries of Byzantium (1261–453), which is known as the Palaiologan era after the name of the ruling dynasty, certain sections of the Hippodrome were used quite rarely. The Hippodrome, which would never regain its former glory, eventually became an abandoned space where peddlers roamed, and people gathered to kill time.

In 1403, when Ruy Gonzales de Clavijo, the ambassador of the king of Castile to Tamerlane arrived in Constantinople, he passed from Pera to Constantinople on a rowboat and asked the emperor for permission to visit the churches and the relics of the city. As he was sightseeing, he also visited the Hippodrome and recorded his impressions in his travelogue. This eyewitness account from 1403 is important as it mentions the sphendone's massive columns and portico, the imperial box, the Egyptian obelisk, and the Serpent column.[38] Hence, we know that these monuments were in place in 1403. In a 1480 drawing, Onofrio Panuinio depicted the substructure of the sphendone and the colonnade above; the Egyptian obelisk and some of the columns on the spina; and two-storey starting gates on the northern side made up of multiple sections.

There were hippodromes in almost all prominent cities of the Roman Empire; however, because cities gradually shrank and lost their ancient characters, starting from the sixth and seventh centuries, with the exception of large cities such as Constantinople, many of these became obsolete and eventually were completely abandoned.[39] Although, at the beginning of the eighth century, due to various epidemics and famine, Constantinople's population dropped to about

---

[37] *O City of Byzantium: Annals of Niketas Choniates*, translated by Harry J. Magoulias (Detroit, MI: Wayne State University Press, 1984), 358 (649, X, book 2).

[38] Ruy Gonzales de Clavijo, *Narrative of the Embassy to the Court of Timour at Samarcand, A.D. 1403–6*, translated by Clements R. Markham (New York: Burt Franklin Publisher, 1970), 29, 34–5. First printed in 1859 for the Hakluyt Society in London.

[39] Warren Treadgold, *A History of the Byzantine State and Society* (Stanford, CA: Stanford University Press, 1997), 279–80.

100,000, the city continued to maintain its ancient identity to a certain extent, and the Hippodrome, which was an important constituent of this, continued to exist. In the eleventh and twelfth centuries, the empire recollected its power, and until the Latin invasion of 1204, the Hippodrome was once again in service. Unlike what happened in other Byzantine cities, the Hippodrome of Constantinople continued its functions until the end of the Middle Ages, which can be explained by the fact that the city was the capital of the Roman Empire, and that its hippodrome was part of the cult of the emperor and of imperial ceremonies.

3 The Architecture of the Hippodrome

Just like the city walls and the Saint Sophia Church, the Hippodrome is one of the major architectural structures of Constantinople that have survived until today, and it is among the most important cultural heritage elements of modern Istanbul. The Hippodrome of Constantinople was modelled after the Circus Maximus in Rome, of which it is, in architectural terms, a smaller scale replica; however, it was built to be glorious and fit for the new capital city of the empire. Based on the present-day ruins, data gathered from excavations, information in Byzantine written sources, representations in mosaics and similar visual materials, the accounts of the travellers visiting the Hippodrome, and well-preserved examples of hippodromes in other regions of the empire, various restitution attempts have been undertaken for the Hippodrome of Constantinople. A three-dimensional restitution project undertaken by architect A. Tayfun Öner, based on the most recent scientific data available, was featured in an exhibition 'Hippodrome/Atmeydanı: A Stage for Istanbul's History', which opened on 15 February 2010 in the Suna and İnan Kıraç Foundation's Pera Museum in Istanbul, and was also published in the catalogue accompanying the exhibition (Figure 2).[40]

Hippodromes are essentially built to accommodate masses of spectators watching chariot races; hence, their architecture has been shaped by these functions. The main elements of the Hippodrome of Constantinople are the long racetrack spilt in the middle with a barrier, the starting gates located on the short side to the north, the rows of benches forming the bleachers and surrounding the track from three sides, and the imperial box located in the centre of the bleachers on the east side.

---

[40] Brigitte Pitarakis, ed. *Hippodrom/Atmeydanı: İstanbul'un Tarih Sahnesi. Hippodrome/Atmeydanı: A Stage for Istanbul's History*, vol. 1, folder 1 (Istanbul: Pera Müzesi Yayınları, 2010).

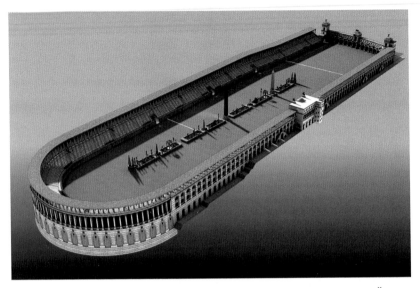

Figure 2 Restitution of the Hippodrome, Byzantium1200.org, by T. Öner

Because no archaeological remains belonging to the Hippodrome have been found on the north side, there is no information about its exact length. However, gathering the available data, J. Bardill has suggested the main measurements of the Hippodrome. According to him, the Hippodrome of Constantinople is mainly a racetrack about 430 metres long and 120 metres wide. The spina in the middle of the racetrack is 230 metres long, the width of the racetrack at the beginning point is 79 metres, while at the south turning point, it measures 76 metres. The total length of the benches is 1,470 metres. Hence, it can be calculated that the Hippodrome could seat approximately 30,000 people.[41] The architectural integrity of the Hippodrome was preserved until the Latin era, which lasted from 1204 to 1261. Quite luckily, three monuments on the spina and the sphendone have survived until the present day.

3.1 The Starting Gates (*Carceres*)

Although the northern boundary of the Hippodrome is not precisely known, when the positions of the Mese, the main avenue of the city, and the Zeuxippus baths, revealed during excavations in 1927–8, are considered, it is assumed that the starting gates were about 430 metres north of the south end of the Hippodrome. The *carceres*, which was in the northern boundary of the Hippodrome, was a monumental entrance gate with multiple floors.

---

[41] Bardill, 'Architecture and Archaeology', 99, table 1.

Competing chariots waited here and jumped onto the racetrack from the twelve gates that opened simultaneously.[42] Every gate had an arch on top and was wide enough to comfortably fit one chariot. An equal number of gates were assigned to the racers of every party. Some races featured four competing chariots, with one rider from each party. In exceptional cases, more than one chariot from each party would race as well. There was a second floor on the entrance structure, which was a gallery with arched windows facing the race area. A twelfth-century fresco located in the Saint Sophia Church of Kiev depicts the *carceres* of the Hippodrome of Constantinople. This mural, made by artists from Constantinople, depicts four arched gates separated with columns, and inside each gate are horse chariots with riders holding whips in the air, waiting and ready to dash off from the gates once they open. The riders in the mural are wearing red, green, white, and blue clothing, which were the colours of the team for which they were competing. The simple, two-winged doors made of thin diagonal bars are as high as the head of the horses. On top of the columns, a second floor supported by arches is visible. On this floor, aligned with the doors below, are windows with open wooden shutters. People looking out of open windows are presumably the officials of the racing teams.

The historian Niketas Khoniates, who witnessed the reign of Emperor Manuel Komnenos, describes the two-storey *carceres* with the bronze horses located on its top.[43] In the middle section of the *carceres*, on top of a tower-like structure, there was a statue of a two-wheeled race chariot, along with its rider and the four horses that pulled it. These four bronze horses were brought from Chios by Theodosius II and were placed on top of the starting gates.[44] Until the thirteenth century, these horses remained in their place on the *carceres*, until they were taken to Venice by the Latins.

3.2 The Racetrack (*Pelma*)

The racetrack is now 4.5–5 metres below the level of the present-day promenade. It was about 80 metres wide and divided in the middle by a wall called the spina, which featured many sculptures and monuments on top. Chariots would complete each tour by going around the spina.

The racetrack had been designed to be wider at its beginning point to prevent the chariots, that would race side by side simultaneously, from getting stuck. At the sphendone section, where the chariots turned, the track was probably made wider as well. This section was the most dangerous part of the race. Chariots entering the curb at high speeds risked being toppled over or colliding into other chariots, and chariot drivers required great dexterity. The finish line was drawn

---

[42] Ibid., 112.   [43] *Annals of Choniates*, 67–8 (119, II, book 3).   [44] *Patria*, 100 (II, 75).

on the surface of the track in white chalk. The racetrack was probably made of rammed earth.

3.3 The Tiers

The tiers of the Hippodrome surrounded the racetrack from three sides, except at the entrance on the north side. There is currently no archaeological data at hand to indicate how many steps high these tiers rose. Robert de Clari, one of the prominent knights of the armies of the Fourth Crusade, which seized Constantinople in 1204, stated that the bleachers were made of thirty to forty steps.[45] However, this seems to be an exaggeration, and it is more logical that there were about twenty steps. These bleachers were placed on a solid infrastructure of graded vaults and corridors. Certain sections of this infrastructure were revealed in excavations conducted in the area. On the uppermost section of the benches that rose step by step was a terrace with a portico that featured sculptures. The spectator section was separated from the racetrack by a high podium wall to protect people seated in the front bleachers from potential accidents. Although this wall separating the benches and the racetrack has not survived, an excellent analogue can be clearly seen in the hippodrome of Leptis Magna in Libya.[46]

The bleachers where the spectators sat were accessed mainly through the gates on the western wall of the Hippodrome. There were three entrances on this side: On the north end, a gate close to the *carceres*, a bit to the south, near the palace of Antiochus, the Antiochus Gate, and across the imperial box, the Necra Gate. The eastern side of the Hippodrome was adjacent to the Great Palace; however, there must have been a gate close to the *carceres*, across the Antiochus Gate, making it possible to access the bleachers. There was also the gate near the sphendone on the south-east side.[47] These five public gates, and the connected staircase-and-corridor system, allowed the bleachers to be easily filled and vacated. Through steps located between the benches, it was possible to access benches located in the top sections. The system was similar to that of modern stadiums.

There was a portico covering the top section of the bleachers. The columns of the portico are visible in some drawings. The front rows of benches, closest to the racetrack and with the best view, had marble seats reserved for senators and other dignitaries. A grandstand in the bleachers was reserved for supporters of the circus factions. Past the starting gates were the main seating areas of the Blues, the Whites, and the Reds, and, close to the sphendone, that of the

---

[45] Rodolphe Guilland, 'The Hippodrome at Byzantium', *Speculum* 23, no. 4 (1948): 679.
[46] Humphrey, *Roman Circuses*, 25.   [47] Bardill, 'Architecture and Archaeology', 115.

Greens.[48] Ambassadors and foreigners who lived in the city could watch the races from their dedicated seating areas in the Hippodrome bleachers. For example, as a result of an agreement made with the emperor in the twelfth century, the Pisans were given a dedicated place.[49] The back rows were for ordinary citizens.

The benches were originally built of wood. This is evident from the fact that the Hippodrome frequently experienced fires and its benches required repairs. According to Byzantine sources, the benches of the Hippodrome were destroyed by fire several times: in 406, 491, 498, and 507 fires damaged the benches, and some repairs were undertaken. The wooden benches which burned down during the Nika Revolt of 532 were replaced with stone benches by Emperor Justinian after the quelling of the revolt. There are no reports of major fires that took place in the Hippodrome following this date.[50] Indeed, Cristoforo Buondelmonti, who visited the city in the fifteenth century, reports that the benches were made of stone. The spectators did not sit directly on the stone, but used pillows, *kilims*, wooden seats, and the like, which they brought along or rented.[51]

In excavations organised in the early twentieth century in and around the Hippodrome, a few steps belonging to the benches were found in situ. A marble bench that was revealed by accident is standing today in the courtyard of the Sultanahmet Mosque, in the section facing the Hippodrome. During restoration efforts undertaken in 2013 in the former Ibrahim Pasha Palace, which serves today as the Turkish and Islamic Arts Museum, certain vaulted remnants were revealed on the ground floor, which turned out to be the infrastructure of the Hippodrome bleachers.[52] The conservation efforts of these ruins have now been completed, and today these are being exhibited in the same museum.

Some sources report that the spectator capacity of the Hippodrome was 80,000–100,000; however, a more realistic estimation made by calculating the total length of the seating areas indicates 30,000.[53] Although it has been claimed that the bleachers were covered with an awning to protect spectators from the rain and sun, there are no archaeological findings and no reliable sources to support this. Rodolphe Guilland believes that this assumption originates from the misinterpretations of certain sections in *The Book of Ceremonies*. According

[48] Alan Cameron, *Porphyrius the Charioteer* (New York: Oxford University Press, 1973), 183–4.
[49] Deno John Geanakoplos, *Byzantium: Church, Society, and Civilization Seen through Contemporary Eyes* (Chicago: University of Chicago Press, 1984), 317.
[50] Guilland, 'Hippodrome', 679.   [51] Ibid., 680.
[52] Engin Akyürek, 'Konstantinopolis Hipodromu', in *Türk ve İslam Eserleri Müzesi, 100 Yıl Önce 100 Yıl Sonra*, edited by Seracettin Şahin, Sevgi Kutluay, and Miyase Çelen, 144–9, figs 1–3 (Ankara: T. C. Kültür ve Turizm Bakanlığı Yayınları, 2014).
[53] Bardill, 'Architecture and Archaeology', 99.

to him, no awning was stretched over the seats of the Hippodrome to shade the spectators.[54] It also seems unlikely that the bleachers, which surrounded the racetrack from three sides and rose about twenty steps high, were covered. But it is known that the top of the imperial box was already covered with an architectural structure. There might have been a cloth spread on top of certain special places where eminent individuals, such as faction leaders, sat. In addition, the wide area that made up the top of the bleachers was covered by a portico supported by columns. There was an official in charge of the setup of the benches of the Hippodrome.[55]

3.4 The Sphendone

The largest architectural structure to survive from the Hippodrome until the present day is the half-rounded part of the racetrack, which forms its southern end. This semi-circular south end, called the sphendone, was built as an artificial terrace, since the land upon which the Hippodrome was located inclined towards the Sea of Marmara in this direction. On top of a very solid infrastructure supported by arches, parallel to the semi-circular racetrack where chariots turned, were bleachers set up in a semicircle. And, in the uppermost section overseeing the Sea of Marmara, there was a scenic platform covered by porticos. The lofty columns which supported the porticos of this section were still visible in the sixteenth century. An anonymous Russian pilgrim, who arrived in Constantinople at the end of the fourteenth century, described the thirty large columns on the sphendone terrace overseeing the Sea of Marmara, and noted that each one had iron rings.[56] These rings were probably for hanging flags announcing upcoming chariot races in the Hippodrome, or they were for attaching a cover on the sphendone terrace. Ruy Gonzales de Clavijo, who visited the Hippodrome in 1403, mentions the thirty-seven gigantic columns in the sphendone, and the porticos they carried:

> On another day the ambassadors went to see a plain called the Hippodrome, where they joust. It is surrounded by white marble pillars, so large that three men can only just span around them, and their height is two lances. They are thirty-seven in number, fixed in very large white marble bases; and above, they were connected by arches going from one to the other, so that a man can walk all around.[57]

---

[54] Guilland, 'Hippodrome', 676–8.

[55] Porphyrogennetos, *Book of Ceremonies*, 803, 805 (book 2, chapter 55).

[56] George P. Majesca, *Russian Travelers to Constantinople in the Fourteenth and Fifteenth Centuries* (Washington, DC: Dumbarton Oaks, 1984), 252.

[57] Clavijo, *Narrative of the Embassy to the Court of Timour at Samarcand,* 34.

These columns also appear in the accounts and in the drawings of certain travellers who visited the city during the Ottoman period, but the reported number varies.

In the infrastructure, radiating from the centre of the curve of sphendone, were twenty-five concentric rooms. From the inside, these rooms opened to a corridor that continued all along the Hippodrome. The large arched openings seen from the outside correspond to these rooms. In the great earthquake of 551, the Hippodrome was damaged and the twenty-five large openings in the sphendone section were walled up in order to strengthen the building, and large piers were built onto the circular corridor.[58] During the Middle Ages, the infrastructure of the sphendone was altered to allow the use of certain sections as a cistern. This large architectural structure is still standing firmly despite the modern construction that exists over it today, and it is one of the largest Byzantine-period structures in the historical peninsula of Istanbul (Figure 3).

After the Latin occupation ended in 1261, the Hippodrome was greatly damaged, and it was no longer possible to hold chariot races there. Smaller-scale tournaments and activities were then organised in the southern half of the Hippodrome, in the sphendone section. The spectators sat in the bleachers of the sphendone section to watch the events. It is known that, during the Byzantine era, some executions were held in the sphendone of the Hippodrome, and that people filled the bleachers to watch in excitement.[59]

Figure 3 Sphendone, photo by E. Akyürek

---

[58] Guilland, 'Hippodrome', 682.   [59] Ibid., 681.

3.5 The Imperial Box (*Kathisma*)

Emperors watched the chariot races from the imperial box, located on the bleachers on the east of the Hippodrome, which had a passage connecting it to the palace. The imperial box was in the section of the bleachers that is the present-day location of the Sultanahmet Mosque and across the Serpent column situated approximately in the middle of the spina. The emperor could pass from his palace directly to his box in the Hippodrome to watch the races. The origin of the imperial box in the Hippodrome of Constantinople can be traced back to a royal enclosure known as the *pulvinar*, which Emperor Augustus had built for himself and his family in the Circus Maximus in Rome.

The *kathisma* was a complex made up of a suite of architectural structures, connecting the Hippodrome with the imperial palace. A balcony-like section visible from the hippodrome was the part of the *kathisma* that was open to the outside. In the inner section, there were probably private rooms in which the emperors rested, prepared, and where their servants and guards were. In *The Book of Ceremonies*, this unit is referred to as the '*kathisma* palace'.[60] The box overlooking the Hippodrome was supported by marble columns, and it was above the place called *stoma* where the imperial guard were located, which was at the same level as the racetrack. This section of the *kathisma* which opened to the Hippodrome was restricted to the emperor and his family, certain high-ranking palace officials, and the private imperial guards. This box, with a throne for the emperor, was the only place where the emperor could be seen by the people gathered in the Hippodrome.

According to the sources, the imperial box had two floors, and its structure featured sculptures of Diocletian and Justinian depicted on horses. Underneath the imperial box was a large, vaulted passageway that provided direct access from the racetrack to the imperial palace. This passage can also be seen on the relief located on the south-west face of the pedestal of the Egyptian obelisk, which depicts the imperial box. It is known that Emperor Theophilos (r. 829–42) used the passage below the imperial box to go on horseback from the Hippodrome directly to the courtyard of the Daphne Palace.[61] In case of a threat, the gates connecting the Hippodrome to the palace were closed. The imperial box has been rendered in relief on four faces of the pedestal of the Egyptian obelisk.

At the beginning of the fifteenth century, enough of the imperial box was still standing that it could be identified. Ruy Gonzales de Clavijo mentions the box sitting on top of piers:

---

[60] Porphyrogennetos, *Book of Ceremonies*, 364–9 (book 1, chapter 73).
[61] Ibid., 507 (appendix to book 1).

In front of these seats, there is a row of pillars, on which is a high seat, raised on four marble pillars, surrounded by other seats, and at each corner there are four images of white marble, the size of a man; and the emperor is accustomed to sit here, when he views the tournaments.[62]

3.6 The Spina (*Euripos*)

The spina, or *euripos*, is a barrier, located in the middle of the racetrack, which it splits in two. The chariots would go around this barrier to complete a tour. Although only three of the many sculptures and monuments on the spina have survived, these make it possible to determine the orientation of both the spina and the racetrack. Naturally, the spina was not a mere wall. According to more realistically executed restitutions, there were rectangular water pools between the monuments and sculptures located on the spina.[63] Unfortunately, no archaeological data concerning the spina were obtained during excavation efforts in the Hippodrome of Constantinople; however, the numerous water conduits and piping found may point to the presence of these pools.[64] Additionally, the fact that remnants indicating the presence of pools have been found in other Roman hippodromes[65] and that some floor mosaics featuring hippodrome depictions showed pools of water on the spina[66] are signs that similar pools could have existed in the spina of the Hippodrome of Constantinople. The water pools on the spina also seem to fit the Hippodrome's symbolism as described by Malalas, who believed the racetrack symbolised '*all land*', while the spina in the centre symbolised '*seas surrounded by land*'.[67] Although there are no precise archaeological data on the length of the spina and its height relative to the racetrack, it is believed that it was about 230 metres long. It is conceivable that it was 1.5–2 metres higher than the ground level of the racetrack.

On either end of the spina, there were three conical columns that served as turning posts (*metae*). These turning posts do not survive; however, they can be

---

[62] Clavijo, *Narrative of the Embassy to the Court of Timour at Samarcand,* 34–5.

[63] Bardill, 'Architecture and Archaeology', 138.

[64] Jonathan Bardill, 'Hippodrom'da Kazılar ve Arkeologlar/Archaeologists and Excavations in the Hippodrome', in *Hippodrom/Atmeydanı*, vol. 1, 83–90 (86).

[65] For example, in the Leptis Magna hippodrome in Libya, rectangular pools of water were found between the monuments on the spina during excavations. See Humphrey, *Roman Circuses*, 38–40.

[66] For example, in the Villa Romana del Casale (Piazza Armerina) in Sicily, rectangular pools can clearly be seen among the monuments on the spina of the hippodrome depicted on the floor mosaics of the palaestra, known as the two-apsed room. In the hippodrome depiction of a 14 × 4 metre ground mosaic, discovered in 1939 by a farmer in the village of Akaki in Nicosia and excavated between 2013 and 2016, the central part of the spina was painted with blue tessera and probably in the form of a water channel.

[67] *Chronicle of Malalas*, 93 (book 7, 175).

clearly seen in the racetrack depiction on the lowest section of the reliefs on the south-west side of the marble base of the Egyptian obelisk (see Figure 8, lower panel). Similarly, the scene from the Great Palace mosaics exhibited in the Istanbul Mosaic Museum shows 'children playing chariot races at the Hippodrome', and these turning posts are seen in the same layout (Figure 4).

4 Monuments and Sculptures

Various monuments and sculptures complemented the architecture of the Hippodrome.[68] The Hippodrome was the most significant public space of the city and all key ceremonies and celebrations were held here. Additionally, it was a locus for spectacular imperial ceremonies, and a propaganda venue for showing off the power of the empire. Hence, it was essential to decorate the Hippodrome with extravagant monuments and sculptures that had symbolic significance. It is known that most of these monuments and sculptures were located on the spina in the middle. The Egyptian obelisk of Pharaoh Thutmose III (r. 1479–25 BCE) and the bronze altar of the temple of Delphi were among the most important monuments of the ancient world. Important symbolic monuments referring to the ancient past of Rome, such as the sculpture of Herakles and the sculpture of the wolf nursing Remus and Romulus, were also brought to Constantinople and placed into the Hippodrome. These sculptures were installed inside the Hippodrome of Constantinople as metaphors to imply that this was the new capital of the world and that the power had been transferred from the previous capital to the new one.[69] As the Hippodrome of Constantinople was modelled after the Circus Maximus in Rome, the design of its monuments was also similar to the originals in Rome.

The three most prominent monuments of the Hippodrome are the Egyptian obelisk, the Walled obelisk, and the Serpent column, which are still standing today in their original locations on the spina.

4.1 The Egyptian Obelisk

The Egyptian obelisk (Figure 5), which is today one of the most glamorous monuments of the Hippodrome was built to honour Pharaoh Thutmose III in 1450 BCE. It was originally located in temple of the god Amon-Ra in Thebes, present-day Karnak. Emperor Constantine I had two obelisks removed from this temple, presumably to bring one to Rome and the other to Constantinople. They

---

[68] Jonathan Bardill, 'Konstantinopolis Hippodromu'nun Anıtları ve Süslemeleri/The Monuments and Decoration of the Hippodrome in Constantinople', in *Hippodrom/Atmeydanı*, vol. 1, 149–84.

[69] Sarah Guberti Bassett, 'The Antiquities in the Hippodrome of Constantinople', *Dumbarton Oaks Papers* 45 (1991): 94.

Figure 4 Children playing the Hippodrome games, photo by E. Akyürek

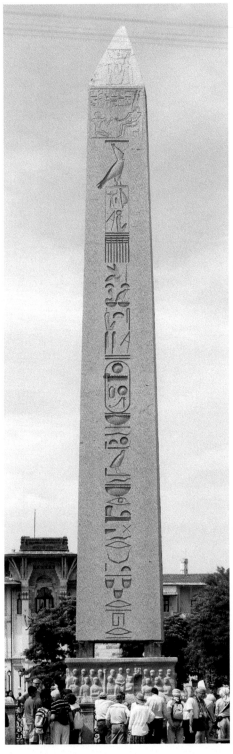

Figure 5 Egyptian obelisk, Gabam Archives, photo by A. Mustafazadeh

were transported over the Nile on rafts, and brought to the port of Alexandria, yet Constantine died before the monuments found their way to his new capital. After his death in 357, his son Constantius II (r. 337–61) sent one of these twin stones to Rome, and had it installed in the Circus Maximus, on the spina right next to the obelisk previously brought from Egypt by Emperor Augustus. Hence, there were two obelisks in the Circus Maximus, Rome's hippodrome, and this constituted a model for subsequent hippodromes. As for the other obelisk, it was brought by Emperor Julian (r. 361–3) from Alexandria to Constantinople, probably in 362, but it was held in the port for about thirty years and could not be installed. The monument was only brought to and installed in its intended place in the Hippodrome in 390, by Emperor Theodosius I. The second obelisk in the Hippodrome of Constantinople is not a monolith but a work of stone masonry. The obelisks in the Circus Maximus and the Hippodrome of Constantinople are positioned identically on the spina.

The obelisk brought to Constantinople was probably broken during transportation, and its original length of 34 metres was reduced to 19.5 metres. The stone is adorned from top to bottom with hieroglyphics, and it appears that the symbols on the bottom are cut. We do not have any information concerning at which stage the obelisk was broken, but it is highly likely that this happened as it was being installed in Constantinople. It was placed on a heightened pedestal, perhaps to compensate for its deficiency to a certain extent and to bring it to the same height as the Walled obelisk on the southern side of the spina. Indeed, it would seem that the pedestal of the obelisk has two levels, and that the second one was added to increase the total height of the monument.

The obelisk made of granite porphyry is sitting on four bronze cubes placed on the pedestal. How this gigantic stone that is not affixed to anything was installed and how it sat on four bronze cubes also surprised Ruy Gonzales de Clavijo, who visited the Hippodrome in the beginning of the fifteenth century:

> on the top of those blocks [marble pedestals] there are four square blocks of copper. On the top of these blocks there is an immense stone, sharp at the end, at least six lances in height. It is not fixed in any way; so that it was marvellous to think how so great a mass of stone, yet so sharp and fine, could have been placed there.[70]

Ruy Gonzales de Clavijo was curious about who erected the stone monument, but he confesses that he never found out because he could not read the Greek language inscription on the pedestal. The installation of the monument was mentioned in the two inscriptions on the base of the obelisk. The Greek inscription on the north-west pedestal reads:

---

[70] Clavijo, *Narrative of the Embassy to the Court of Timour at Samarcand*, 35.

Only the Emperor Theodosius daring to uprise the four-sided pillar, ever
lying a burden on the earth, called Proclus to his aid, and so huge a pillar stood
up in thirty-two days.[71]

On the south-east pedestal of the monument, there is another inscription in
Latin. What is interesting is that this inscription has been written from the voice
of the obelisk:

Difficult once, I was ordered to be obedient to the serene master[s] and, after
the tyrant[s] had been extinguished, to carry the palm. All things cede to
Theodosius and his undying issue. Thus I, defeated and tamed in thirty days,
when Proclus was judge, was raised to the skies above.[72]

Mentioned in both inscriptions is the prefect of Constantinople, Proclus,
a man of Lycian origin, who was tasked by the emperor with the installation
of the monument.

The other two surfaces of the lower pedestal illustrate the transportation and
the installation of the obelisk, and the chariot races in the Hippodrome. The
north-east side shows the obelisk lying on the ground, as it is being hoisted
through the many ropes attached to it. What is remarkable about this relief is that
it renders the hieroglyphs on the obelisk just as they are. On the lower section,
many workers are shown cranking jacks to raise the monument into place. The
figure standing on an elevated pedestal with one hand on his hip and the other
extended towards the laborers as if providing instructions is probably the
praefectus Proclus.

The south-western side of the lower pedestal depicts the chariot races in the
Hippodrome. The two obelisks can be seen standing in the central spina. At
either end of the spina, the three conical columns designating the turning points
can be seen. Four *quadriga* chariots are racing, most probably representing the
four parties. In addition, on the other side of the spina, two horsemen are
depicted, and on the spina itself, certain figures are depicted, which are probably
sculptures.

The four sides of the cubical upper pedestal depict Emperor Theodosius I,
watching the races in the Hippodrome from his imperial box. On the north-
western face (Figure 6), the large figure in the centre is Theodosius I. To his
left is the Western Roman Emperor Valentinian II (r. 375–92), and to his right
are his sons Arcadius and Honorius (r. 395–423). The top of the box is covered
with a roof supported by columns while the balcony-like front section is
closed with decorated marble slabs. The front row of figures on either side
of the box are the dignitaries of the palace, while the armed guards are

---

[71] English text after Bardill, 'Monuments', 156.   [72] Ibid.

Figure 6 Pedestal of the obelisk, north-west face, Gabam Archives, photo by
A. Mustafazadeh

depicted in the back. Underneath the imperial box, captured barbarians are
pictured kneeling in front of the emperor and presenting him their gifts. On the
left side, the Persians can be distinguished by their typical headgear, while on
the right Germanic tribesmen can be spotted wearing furs. This image repre-
sents the universal domination of the emperor over the barbaric peoples in the
east and west.

On the face of the pedestal to the south-east (Figure 7), in the middle,
Theodosius is depicted in the box covered with a straight roof, holding
a wreath, with family members, possibly his children, on his sides. The wreath
was meant to be given to the winner of the chariot race. On either side of the
group, again, are the dignitaries of the palace and the guards. In the lower
section of the box are the dancers and musicians who performed to entertain the
spectators between chariot races. On either end, two musical instruments
similar to an organ are noticeable. Above the musicians and dancers, a large
crowd of spectators is depicted in two rows.

On the south-west face of the pedestal (Figure 8), in the middle, the emperor
is shown sitting with three individuals underneath an arched roof supported by
columns. On either side of the box are two civilian officials standing with
shield-bearing soldiers next to them. From the upper section of the imperial
box separated with a balustrade, the descending steps of a wide staircase can be
seen. There are two tall figures standing on either side of the steps. The figures

Figure 7 Pedestal of the obelisk, south-east face, Gabam Archives, photo by
A. Mustafazadeh

sitting in the two rows on the sides of the staircase are probably officials. Just
below the steps, there is an arched gate.

On the fourth face in the north-east (Figure 9), the emperor is sitting
underneath the arch supported by columns, and there are figures on both
sides. Palace dignitaries are depicted as three figures on either side of the box,
and in the back are guards holding lances. Underneath the box where the
emperor is, a wide vaulted passage can be seen. Judging from their clothing,
the figures lined up in two rows on either side of the passage are dignitaries from
the palace or high-level functionaries. This wide vaulted passage is probably the
one mentioned in the sources, leading directly from the racetrack into the
courtyard of the imperial palace.

Figure 8 Pedestal of the obelisk, south-west face, Gabam Archives, photo by A. Mustafazadeh

Figure 9 Pedestal of the obelisk, north-east face, Gabam Archives, photo by A. Mustafazadeh

Figure 10 Serpent column, photo by E. Akyürek

4.2 The Serpent Column

Located on the same line to the south of the obelisk, the Serpent column is a bronze monument depicting three intertwined serpents (Figure 10). The top of the monument is now broken, but originally it was a column made of the three intertwined snake bodies, the three snake heads diverged to three different directions, and there was a golden tripod sitting on top. This monument was made in 479 BCE to commemorate the victory of the union of Greek city-states in the Platea war against the Persians, by melting the bronze weapons of the vanquished soldiers, and it was presented as a 'votive offering' to the god Apollo in his temple at Delphi. Excavations conducted at the base of the Serpent column revealed that the names of the Greek city-states fighting the Persian army in Platea were engraved on the lower section. This altar was brought to Constantinople by Constantine in the fourth century, 750 years after its erection, and was installed on the spina in the middle of the

Hippodrome.[73] This monument was also one of the most significant, prestigious symbols of the ancient world. Because it represented the victory of the Greeks over the Persians, it was seen as a symbol of order over chaos, of civilisation over barbarism. Since Delphi was considered the holy centre of the ancient world, this monument also represented the centre of the world. Hence, Constantine brought this monument to Constantinople, the new capital of the Roman Empire, because it was the new centre of the world.[74] Additionally, this monument had a symbolic meaning for the city, because the defeat of the Persians in 479 BCE ended the Persian dominance over the city of Byzantium – later Constantinople – that continued since the sixth century BCE, and the city earned its independence. Therefore, the bronze monument was placed in the exact centre of the spina, and the two obelisks were installed on either side at an equal distance. This position is an indication of the special significance of the monument.

There is no information as to when the golden tripod on top of the column went missing; however, at the time when Constantine brought the monument to Constantinople in the fourth century, this golden tripod was probably not there. For centuries, Greeks, Romans, Byzantines, and later Ottomans ascribed holy properties to this pagan monument, and it was considered to have healing and apotropaic powers. In time, the pagan meaning of the monument was forgotten, and it became more of a talisman. The armies of the Fourth Crusade that invaded Constantinople in 1204, mercilessly plundered the city, and they removed all of the bronze sculptures in the Hippodrome and the bronze plating of the Walled obelisk; however, they were reluctant to touch this bronze monument.

Accounts of travellers visiting the city, accounts of Russian pilgrims, and written and visual sources from the Ottoman period attest that the snake heads were intact until the eighteenth century. Four Russian pilgrims visiting Constantinople between 1349 and 1422 mention the Hippodrome, and especially the Serpent column.[75] One of these, Ignatius, reports seeing the Serpent column with three snake heads. Another pilgrim, Zosima, saw the three snake heads in place, and reported that their mouths were open, and their teeth were visible. Zosima states that venom was sealed inside the column and that any city dweller bit by a snake would be cured if they touched the monument. The Serpent column was significant as a folkloric element both during the Byzantine era and later, and it was considered a talisman that protected the city from

---

[73] *Patria*, 103 (II, 79).

[74] Rolf Strootman, 'The Serpent Column: The Persistent Meanings of a Pagan Relic in Christian and Islamic Constantinople', *Material Religion* 10, no. 4 (2014): 434–6.

[75] Majesca, *Russian Travelers*, 250–4.

snakes and harmful insects. Ruy Gonzales de Clavijo, who visited the city in 1403 and saw the monument, had this to say:

> and between those columns there are three copper figures of serpents. They are twisted like a rope, and they have three heads, with open mouths. It is said that these figures were of serpents who were put there, on account of an enchantment which was affected. The city was used to be infested by many serpents, and other evil animals, which killed and poisoned men; but an emperor performed an enchantment over these figures, and serpents have never done any harm to the people of the city, since that time.[76]

Only 5.5 metres of the bronze column composed of the three intertwined snake bodies stands today. The snake heads were somehow broken and destroyed. Some sources state that following his seizure of the city, Mehmed II the Conqueror (r. 1451–81) broke the lower jaw of one of the snake heads with his mace as a show of strength, yet this has not been firmly attested. Ottoman written sources state that the snake heads fell and broke on their own accord at midnight on 20 October 1700.[77] One of the snake heads was found in 1842 during Fossati's work,[78] it is now on display in the Istanbul Archaeological Museums (Figure 11).

Some water conduits were revealed during excavation work undertaken around the monument, and it was concluded that the monument may have served as a fountain for a while. This proposition may also suggest that the Crusaders who removed and melted the bronze plating of the Walled obelisk and all bronze sculptures did not dismantle this bronze monument because they were using the fountain.

4.3 The Walled Obelisk

In place of a second obelisk, as in the Circus Maximus, in Constantinople, a walled obelisk was built in imitation of the Karnak obelisk, and this was covered with bronze plating. Both obelisks were installed to match the positions of the ones in the hippodrome of Rome.

The 32-metre-high second obelisk in the spina of the Hippodrome was built using cut stone masonry (Figure 12). Perhaps this obelisk was built with the intention of being later replaced with a monolith monument like the granite

---

[76] Clavijo, *Narrative of the Embassy to the Court of Timour at Samarcand*, 35.

[77] Victor Louis Ménage, 'The Serpent Column in Ottoman Sources', *Anatolian Studies* 14 (1964): 172–3.

[78] Wolfgang Müller-Wiener, *Bildlexikon zur Topographi Istanbuls: Byzantion, Konstantinupolis, Istanbul bis zum Beginn des 17 Jahrhunderts* (Tübingen: Ernst Wasmuth Verlag, 1977), 69. Brothers Gaspare and Guiseppe Fossati, Swiss architects, constructed/renovated several buildings in Constantinople between 1841 and 1848, including the renovation of Saint Sophia.

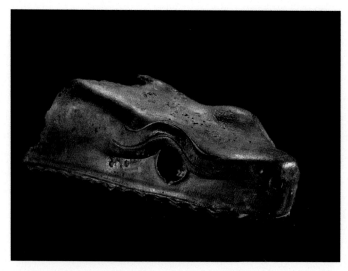

Figure 11 Bronze head of one of the serpents, Istanbul Archaeological Museums

Figure 12 Walled obelisk, photo by E. Akyürek

obelisk brought from Egypt. Although many of the stones of the present monument were renewed in the nineteenth century, as can be seen from the many holes on the original stones, the obelisk was covered in bronze plates. It was probably built in response to the installation of a second obelisk in the Circus Maximus in Rome in 357. The Walled obelisk was repaired by Emperor Constantine VII Porphyrogennetos in the tenth century, and its bronze plates were replaced. This repair was recorded with an inscription on the base of the Walled obelisk. The inscription compares the monument with the large sculpture located in Rhodes, and indicates that it was covered with bronze plates:

> The four-sided marvel of the uplifted, wasted by time, now Constantine the Emperor, whose son is Romanus, the glory of the kingship, restores better than the ancient spectacle. For the Colossus was a wonder once in Rhodes, and this is now a brazen wonder here.[79]

This bronze plating was removed and melted during the Latin occupation, and it was used to make weapons and mint coins. After the Latin era, these bronze plates were never renewed.

At the end of the nineteenth century, some stones of the monument were missing, and its upper third, which was dangerously bent, was dismantled and reconstructed. During the repair, the missing pieces were probably replaced with the stones that fell from the city walls around Topkapı.[80]

4.4 Sculptures

Following Constantine I's proclamation of Constantinople as the new capital of the Roman Empire in 330, important monuments and sculptures were transported to the city from all over the Roman world, and hundreds of these found their new homes in the public areas of the city. The Hippodrome, which was the most important of these spaces, was a locus for all types of sculptures and monuments. As the construction of the Hippodrome was completed, Constantine started the process of systematically decorating it with monuments, and subsequent emperors continued this practice.[81]

In addition to the two obelisks and the Serpent column monuments that are still standing today, the Hippodrome of Constantinople featured many sculptures. Although very few have survived until the present age, sources provide some hints and information as to what they were. The forty-eight sculptures that

---

[79] English text after Bardill, 'Monuments', 151.
[80] There are two documents in Ottoman archives, one dated 1889 (DH.MTK 1607–65) and the other dated 1894 (I. Hus 31–57). I would like to thank Ayhan Han who identified and translated these documents and brought them to my attention.
[81] Dagron, *L'hippodrome de Constantinople*, 94.

used to stand in the Hippodrome can be listed thanks to information gathered from various written and visual sources. Among these were sculptures of emperors such as Augustus, Diocletian, Justinian, and Anastasius; famous chariot racers such as Porphyrius, Faustinus, Julian, and Constantine, and some other illustrious athletes; pagan gods such as Zeus, whose title was '*hippias*' in connection to horses, and the goddess Artemis, the protectress of horses; pagan demigods such as Herakles, symbolising power and victory; Scylla, in mermaid form and representing whirlpools at sea, who was associated with struggle; heroes such as the Dioscuri who were role models epitomising strength and virtuous behaviour; and horses; statues of animals such as wolves, wild boars, and geese; and tripods shaped like victory cups.[82]

One of the sculptures in the Hippodrome was the gigantic bronze statue of Herakles.[83] The Byzantine historian Niketas Khoniates describes this statue in such detail that one can visualise it:

> Also overturned was Herakles, mighty in his mightyness. . . the lion skin which was thrown over him looked terrifying even in bronze . . . He was thick in the chest and broad in the shoulders, with curly hair; fat in the buttocks, strongin the arms, he was an incomparable masterpiece fashioned from the first to the lastby the hands of Lysimachos and portrayed in the magnitude which the artist must have attributed to the real Herakles; the statue was so large that it took a cord the size of a man's belt to go around the thumb, and the shin was the size of a man.[84]

Another group of bronze sculptures in the Hippodrome depict Scylla,[85] who is described in Greek mythology as a terrifying monster. Although there is no information about the form of these sculptures, another work of art known as the Scylla group, found in 1957 in the Sperlonga villa of Emperor Tiberius (r. 14–37 CE) along the coast between Rome and Naples in Italy, provides some clues. In Greek mythology, Scylla is a monster guarding a narrow water passageway and attacking passing ships; and in the group of sculptures in Italy, she was portrayed as a colossal human woman from the waist up with six long necks emerging from her middle section, each terminating in dog heads with sharp teeth, and her lower half was in the shape of a fishtail. The Scylla group of bronze sculptures in the Hippodrome of Constantinople were probably inspired by this famous statue in Italy.

---

[82] For the list of eighty-four statues, see Bardill, 'Monuments', 180–2. See also Bassett, 'Antiquities in the Hippodrome', 89–91. According to Bassett, sources document at least twenty-five antiquities, most of which were figural sculptures, ibid. 88.

[83] Dagron, *L'hippodrome de Constantinople*, 103–4.

[84] *Annals of Choniates*, 358–9 (650, X, book 2).

[85] Dagron, *L'hippodrome de Constantinople*, 104–5.

Another statue in the Hippodrome was that of the Calydonian boar. In Greek mythology, the goddess Artemis dispatched a wild boar to ravage the Calydon region in Aetolia because its king refused to honour her during the ceremonies organised for divinities. The wild boar, which caused a great deal of damage in the Calydon region, was killed in a hunt attended by many heroes.

During the excavations carried out at the Hippodrome, numerous sculptures, ceramics, and other small objects were found. Today, many of these works are in the Istanbul Archaeological Museums. Two among these are significant because of their connection to the Hippodrome. One is the naked torso of an acrobat doing a handstand on four small pillars. This stone sculpture has been dated to the eleventh century. The other one is the column capital with an acanthus leaf strip at the bottom, featuring a high relief of Pegasus, whose wings touch the four corners. The horse heads appear to be coming out of the capital and have been skilfully crafted. A bronze goose statue found near the Hippodrome is on display at the British Museum in London.

Most of these statues and monuments were on the spina, but it is known that there were sculptures on the entrance door and within the imperial box. On top of the starting gates, there was a *quadriga* statue complete with its rider and four bronze horses. These four bronze horses, which were made by the Greek sculptor Lysippos, were removed and taken to Venice by the armies of the Fourth Crusade and placed in San Marco Square. Recently, the horse statues in the outdoor area have been replaced with replicas, and the originals are now being displayed indoors. This rich collection of sculptures was preserved for the most part until 1204, until the time the Latins plundered and damaged them.

Two sculpture pedestals, which offer very valuable data about the Hippodrome races and the racers, are today in the Istanbul Archaeological Museums. These are the pedestals of the statues belonging to the famous chariot racer Porphyrius.[86] These bronze statues standing on the spina probably shared the same fate as other bronze sculptures during the Latin occupation, but their marble pedestals have survived. One was found and placed in the museum in 1845, and the other in 1963. Both pedestals have reliefs on all four sides. As both pedestals have very similar iconographies, it would be enough to mention details pertinent to the so-called old pedestal.

Its dimensions are 2.85 metres in height, 1 metre in width, and 0.85 metres in depth. The fractured upper part of the front of the base was restored and completed; however, the inscription has disappeared completely (Figure 13). The charioteer Porphyrius is standing in the chariot drawn by four horses, and he is depicted from the front holding a victory wreath in his right hand, and

---

[86] For charioteer Porphyrius, see Cameron, *Porphyrius.*

Figure 13 Pedestal of the Porphyrius sculpture, front, Istanbul Archaeological Museums

a palm branch in his left. On the platform where the chariot is standing, the names of the four horses have been provided: Aristides, Palaistiniarkhes, Purros, and Euthynikos. On either side of Porphyrius are Nike figures, and on the bottom are two nude cupids holding the horses by their reins. The inscription under this panel indicates that Porphyrius passed everyone in the race, and that he changed horses, and competed again in the second race. Underneath this inscription, the changing of four horses led by their reins has been depicted.

The inscription on the top section of the left face of the pedestal is partially legible (Figure 14). The entire text of the inscription as it appears in the Planudean Anthology, Epigram 340 is as follows:

Figure 14 Pedestal of the Porphyrius sculpture, left side, Istanbul
Archaeological Museums

To others when they have retired, but to Porphyrius alone while still racing,
did the Emperor give this honour. For often he drove his own horses to victory
and then took in hand the team of his adversary and was again crowned.
Hence arouse a keen rivalry on the part of the Greens, hence a shout of
applause for him, O King who will give joy both to Blues and to Greens.[87]

This inscription indicates that the statue of Porphyrius was erected while he
was still alive, and that once they won races with their own horses, famous
racers would race with the horse of their adversaries.

---

[87] Aleksandr A. Vasiliev, 'The Monument of Porphyrius in the Hippodrome at Constantinople',
Dumbarton Oaks Papers 4 (1948): 36.

The panel below the inscription again shows Porphyrius standing on a *quadriga* and holding a wreath and a palm branch in the same way. On this face, the horses are depicted not frontally but as profiles. Above the horses, we see once more their inscribed names: Nicopolimos, Padiatos, Purros, and Euntunikes. Underneath this panel, there is another inscription:

> Faction of the Greens, I do not care, give us Porphyrius, in order that those whom Porphyrius pleased [by wining] for the Blue, he may also please for the Green, if he puts on the costume [of the Green].[88]

This inscription reveals that some famous racers competed both for the Greens and the Blues, and that they wore the colour of the faction that they were competing for.

The panel in the lower section shows the victorious Porphyrius standing on the benches of the Hippodrome, acclaimed by the spectators. The benches and the steps between them are also visible.

The iconography of the right face of the pedestal is very similar to the left face. The inscription on the upper right side of the base, which is only partially legible, reads:

> The sculptor exactly portrayed in bronze Porphyrius himself, fashioning him as if alive. But who shall mould his grace, his races, his inspired tricks of his craft, and victory he never varied?[89]

This inscription reveals that the Porphyrius statue on this pedestal was cast in bronze. In the relief underneath the inscription, Porphyrius, similar to other depictions, is shown standing on the *quadriga* and holding the wreath of triumph and a palm branch. The inscription underneath this panel is so damaged that it is no longer legible. On the panel at the very bottom, similar to the panel on the left face, spectators have been depicted standing on the benches of the Hippodrome and cheering in support of their team. These scenes of acclamations on either face provide important information about the seating arrangements in the Hippodrome.

On the back of the pedestal (Figure 15), Porphyrius is depicted standing and dressed in a racer's costume. The inscribed upper part is completely broken. Again, he is holding a wreath of triumph and a palm branch. On either side of him are nude cupid figures. The figure to his left is holding a whip. The bronze statue that once stood on the pedestal was probably depicting a standing figure in frontal pose and wearing a racer costume, as seen in this relief. These sculpture pedestals provide important information concerning the Hippodrome racers.

---

[88] Ibid., 36–7.

[89] Ibid., 37. The inscription later appears on the epigram 342 from the Planudian Anthology.

Figure 15 Pedestal of the Porphyrius sculpture, back side, Istanbul
Archaeological Museums

5 The Hippodrome as the Ceremonial Setting of the City

Many historians believe that Constantinople had three important centres: the
cathedral of the city – Saint Sophia – and the adjacent patriarchal palace, which
represented religious authority and belonged to God; the imperial palace and the
Senate, which represented civil authority and belonged to the emperor; and the
Hippodrome, which represented the populace of the city and belonged to them.
Indeed, this was a space where the people gathered, watched chariot races and

various entertainments, and where the emperor and the people faced each other. In a sense, it was an area representing the people in the face of the civilian authority, and the emperor in the face of people.

Located at the eastern end of Constantinople, this trio indeed constituted the political, religious, and social centre of the city. The Hippodrome was the largest public space of the city, where the people gathered and faced the emperor, and which had social and political functions in addition to the sports and the entertainments. The people gathered here to watch the races and the entertainments and found an opportunity to voice to the emperor their wishes and their complaints. Sometimes, people let out politically charged acclamations in favour of the emperor and prominent administrators, and at other times they broke out in acts of protests that could get violent. The Hippodrome was also a ceremonial centre where the emperor displayed his power, promulgated his propaganda, and sought the support of his people.

The Hippodrome was an important public space in terms of the cult of the emperor. The ceremonies held here to demonstrate the power and the hegemony of the empire made up an important part of the ceremonies held in the city. In this venue, emperors were proclaimed, and public coronations took place. Ceremonies were held to celebrate notable events involving the imperial family, such as marriages or a prince's birth, and races were organised, and these events were announced to the people. Through a parade in the Hippodrome, victorious emperors and commanders displayed the war spoils and the slaves that they acquired, and they celebrated and announced their victories to the public. Foreign ambassadors were invited to the Hippodrome to watch chariot races and ceremonies, so that they could experience the crushing power of the empire. In addition, some public executions were held in the Hippodrome to serve as deterrences.[90]

During the early Byzantine period, the chariot races, the entertainments, and the ceremonies held in the Hippodrome were, as the continuation of the Roman tradition, geared more towards sports and entertainment; they were partially pagan, and got violent at times. Malalas relates that chariot races in Ancient Rome involved violence: 'factions were very hostile towards each other in Rome'.[91] Malalas, who lived in the sixth century, was of course referring to a few hundred years earlier, yet this proclivity to violence existed to a certain extent in his age as well. Despite the objection of the Church, the pagan ceremonial elements continued to exist during the early Byzantine

---

[90] Charles Diehl, 'The Byzantine Civilization' in *The Cambridge Medieval History, Vol. 4: The Eastern Roman Empire (717–1453),* edited by Joseph R. Tanner, Charles W. Previté-Orton, and Zachary N. Brooke (Cambridge: Cambridge University Press, 1927), 759.

[91] *Chronicle of Malalas*, 94 (book 7, 176).

period. Two ceremonies, which according to Byzantine-era sources took place to commemorate the anniversary of the foundation of the city, could constitute examples of the continuation of pagan influence during the early period: on the occasion of chariot races held for the anniversary of the establishment of the city, 11 May, Constantine I ordered that his own statue that held the *tyche* of the city[92] – which he called an anthouse – in its right hand, be brought to the Hippodrome on a *quadriga* accompanied by soldiers dressed in cloaks and boots, and holding torches. Once the chariot completed one lap and stopped in front of the imperial box, it was supposed to salute the statue of Constantine, the reigning emperor at the time, and the *tyche* of the city. Malalas reports that this tradition continued into his own lifetime.[93] During the reign of Theodosius I, the citizens organised a specific show in the Hippodrome. On a *quadriga* in the imperial palace stood the statue of a female chariot racer, which was probably the *tyche* of the city. Everyone entered the Hippodrome dressed in white cloaks, holding torches, and carrying this chariot with the statue of the woman up to the *stoma* in front of the imperial box. This ceremony recurred every year on the anniversary of the founding of Constantinople.[94]

Of course, at every phase of the city's history, the Hippodrome continued to be a venue where the people of the city watched sports and where festivals and various forms of entertainment were held; however, eventually, the importance of the imperial ceremonies increased, and these became more formalised and detailed affairs serving the cult of the emperor. By the tenth century, Hippodrome races were completely integrated into the imperial ceremonies. The leaders of the circus factions found their place among the palace hierarchy, and the chariot races and other entertainment of the late antique era, which occasionally contained vicious violence, were, in a manner of speaking, domesticated. These ceremonies were extremely lengthy, rigidly formalised affairs primarily aiming to praise the emperor, and to demonstrate his power. *The Book of Ceremonies* by Constantine Porphyrogennetos[95] covers in detail the rules of the chariot races, their calendar and organisation, and the imperial ceremonies held in the Hippodrome, and in this context indicates how important they were for the empire. This highly consistent text from the tenth century is a relatively reliable source and possibly shows that the standardised practices it describes had begun in the previous century.[96] Constantine Porphyrogennetos explains

---

[92]   *Tyche*, which means 'luck' in Greek was the patron deity of a city that governed its fortune and protected its prosperity.

[93]   *Chronicle of Malalas*, 175 (book 13, 322).   [94]   *Patria*, 109 (II, 87).

[95]   Porphyrogennetos, *Book of Ceremonies*, 303–64 (book 1, chapters 68–73).

[96]   Dagron, *L'hippodrome de Constantinople*, 23.

that his book covered the Hippodrome ceremonies in painstaking detail because of a desire to standardise them so that they could be transferred to future generations without undergoing change:

> The delightful spectacle of the pleasure of the Hippodrome festival is evident to everyone, and the precise and harmonious organisation and coordination of the various orders in it. Therefore it is also absolutely necessary to leave behind this record for the generations to come indicating the specific insignia of each of them, and the variation in dress and the amount of the customary gift which each of them deposits with the *praipositoi* for the post to which he is assigned, because the *praipositoi* have complete authority over them and control of good order, and they follow closely the ancient format without change.[97]

The race started with long and elaborate ceremonies, and every step of this process such as the preparation of the emperor, the emperor greeting the factions one by one from the imperial box, the emperor initiating the ceremonies, the preparation of the horses, the chariot racers greeting the emperor and the spectators, and the acclamation in favour of the victorious racer – each involved its own elaborate ritual.

The emperor walking out of his palace and facing the people in his Hippodrome box was a long ritual.[98] When the emperor arrived at the *kathisma* palace, the master of ceremonies would tell the *praepositus* that everything was ready, and the *praepositus* would notify the emperor. The emperor would descend the stone steps to the bedchamber and don his imperial tunic called *chalamys*. After he put on his crown, the patricians (high-ranking dignitaries) and the *strategoi* (army generals) met him, and these individuals stepped outside into the box first, followed by the emperor, who was standing in the threshold.

The rituals that accompanied the coronation of Anastasius are described in *The Book of Ceremonies,* they constituted a detailed illustration of the ceremonies held for the proclamation of emperors. After the death of Zeno (r. 474–5 and 476–91), the widowed empress married Anastasius, which made it possible for him to become emperor. After being sworn in at the palace, Anastasius passed to the Hippodrome. The lances and the standards of the soldiers in the *stoma* underneath the imperial box were facing down. Honouring a Roman tradition, Anastasius was raised on a shield by soldiers. Lances fitted with pennants and standards were raised, and the emperor descended from the shield and moved to the section of the palace known as the covered Hippodrome[99] to

---

[97] Porphyrogennetos, *Book of Ceremonies*, 807 (book 2, chapter 56, R. 807).

[98] Ibid., 364–5 (book 1, chapter 73).

[99] Despite being mentioned several times in *The Book of Ceremonies*, it is not clear where the 'Covered hippodrome' was in the imperial palace.

wear his imperial regalia. The patriarch dressed him in the imperial *chalamys*, and he placed the crown onto his head. The emperor then appeared in the imperial box again to greet the crowds. All the bleachers shouted out 'Augustus, the revered one'. The emperor delivered a speech and, following this, the acclamations continued.[100] Theophanes also describes how on 2 October 811 Michael I Rangabe (r. 811–13) was coronated in the Hippodrome and declared emperor.[101]

The Golden Hippodrome Festival, held during the seasonal opening of the chariot races, is also described in detail in *The Book of Ceremonies*. Before the emperor appeared in front of the people, preparations in the form of long rituals were underway in the palace. Meanwhile, the chariots would go into the Hippodrome and take position next to their teams. The supporters of the teams sat in their reserved places in the bleachers, while other spectators filled up the benches on the top sections. When notified that everything was ready, the emperor would step out of his palace room into the Hippodrome box. This also involved some rituals. In the box, he would stand in front of his throne to greet the supporters of all parties and spectators by crossing them. First, he would greet those sitting in the middle section, second, the *deme* of the Blue faction, and third, the *deme* of the Greens.[102] Following this, he would sit on his throne. Meanwhile, the people and the soldiers would cheer him. As the acclamations died down, following the emperor's cue, the *praepositus* called the patricians and the *strategoi* to the imperial box, and these individuals appeared at the box in the order dictated by their rank. Then the races began. After the first four races, there was a break and the emperor returned to the palace. Along with his eminent invitees, he sat at the banquet table and afterwards rested until everything in the Hippodrome was ready. The same ceremonies were repeated for the four afternoon races.[103]

Following a victory, prisoners of war and looted goods were shown off in ceremonies also held at the Hippodrome. In a parade held at the Hippodrome, Justinian's general Belisarius (500–65), who had returned from North Africa victorious, displayed the prisoners of war and the loot that he had acquired.[104] *The Book of Ceremonies* describes these parades at length. The cortege entering the Hippodrome racetrack from the starting gates were headed by armed troops with their lances facing up. The plunder and spoils followed these, then the

---

[100] Porphyrogennetos, *Book of Ceremonies*, 422–3 (book 1, chapter 92).
[101] *Chronicle of Theophanes*, 677 (494).
[102] *Demes (demoi)* literally means the people, but here it refers to the members of the circus factions racing at the Hippodrome.
[103] Porphyrogennetos, *Book of Ceremonies*, 303–9 (book 1, chapter 68).
[104] Theophanes states that among the prisoners, Vandals attracted attention with their long stature and strong physiques. *Chronicle of Theophanes*, 295 (200).

slaves would take part in the parade, and at the very end would be horses and camels, if any were captured. If there were a lot of loot and slaves, these would be paraded in two lines, otherwise they would be in a single line; they would be lined up from the entrance gate to the turning point. When everything was ready, the *praepositus* would notify the emperor, who would then take his place in his box and salute the factions by crossing them three times; and in response, the supporters would recite their acclamations. Once the emperor was seated in his throne, he would put on his crown and the ceremony would begin. As the entire cortege passed in front of the imperial box, choruses would sing chants of victory. As they paraded in front of the emperor, on cue, the slaves would fall flat, and lances adorned with pennants would be lowered to salute the emperor. If the emperor felt gracious, the slaves were allowed to watch the chariot races from the steps located below the bleachers of the Greens.[105]

Important events involving the imperial family, such as the marriage of the emperor or the birth of a prince, were also celebrated and announced through chariot races and ceremonies organised in the Hippodrome. Emperor Theodosius celebrated his wedding with a chariot race in the Hippodrome.[106] The birth of a prince in the purple room[107] also counted as an opportunity for a Hippodrome ceremony. Upon the order of the emperor, a flag was flown in the Hippodrome announcing that races were to be held. And on the fifth day of the birth, a total of 200 persons selected by the *praepositus*: fifty military troops, fifty individuals from each of the two factions, and fifty individuals from the administrators of the city, cheered in the Hippodrome for the emperor, the empress, and the newly born, repeating the name of baby prince.[108]

Sometimes, chariot races and celebrations would be organised in the Hippodrome for foreign emissaries visiting. During the reign of Constantine VII (913–59), a festival was organised in the Hippodrome and chariot races were held for the Arab (Saracen) mission which was visiting Constantinople to discuss a peace treaty and an exchange of prisoners. The supporters of the four factions sat in the areas reserved for them, which were ornamented with colourful pieces of cloth. The bleachers of the Greens and Blues were decorated with pink damask curtains, while those of the Whites and the Reds had reddish-purple ones. Singers from the church of the Holy Apostles and Saint Sophia sat in front of the spectator benches. After the chariot races, dancers performed accompanied by music.[109] In

---

[105] Porphyrogennetos, *Book of Ceremonies*, 612–15 (book 2, chapter 20).
[106] *Chronicon Paschale*, 68 (421).
[107] The purple room was in the emperor's palace. A child born in the prophyr room (they were called prophyrogennetos) indicates that their father was the emperor at the time of their birth.
[108] Porphyrogennetos, *Book of Ceremonies*, 617 (book 2, chapter 21).
[109] Ibid., 588–90 (book 2, chapter 15).

549, an interesting event took place: on 13 October, while races were being held in the Hippodrome, the Indian emissary to Constantinople entered the Hippodrome with an elephant. According to Theophanes, this exotic animal later escaped from the place it was kept, and caused damage and deaths in the city.[110]

The greeting of the chariot racers at the beginning of the races and afterwards was also a complicated and lengthy ritual; in addition to the racer – even more – it was the emperor and the empress who were praised. A short sample from the lengthy cheers delivered to ensure the victory of the racers may provide an idea about the form and the duration of these ritual. First, the cheerleader of the bleachers started the acclamation with praises, and the crowd followed suit by repeating:

- Cheerleader: 'Welcome, appointee of the benefactors.'
- Crowd: 'Welcome, welcome, welcome!'
- Cheerleader: 'May the faith of the emperors be victorious.'
- The crowd repeated this, three times.
- Cheerleader: 'May the faith of the Augustai be victorious.'
- The crowd repeated 'Of the Augustai!' three times.
- Cheerleader: 'May the faith of the city be victorious.'
- The crowd repeated 'Of the City!' three times.
- Cheerleader: 'May the faith of the Greens (or Blues) be victorious.'
- The crowd: 'The Greens (or Blues), The Greens (or Blues)!'[111]

As the winning chariot racer advanced to get his award from the emperor, supporters of both teams let out the 'be victorious' slogan, addressed both to the charioteer and to the emperor.

In general, the populace expressed their desires and complaints in the Hippodrome, in front of the emperor. This would sometimes occur in a peaceful manner and take the shape of acclamations also featuring political messages, at other times this could turn into strong protests and even uprisings. Indeed, many uprisings in Constantinople started in the Hippodrome before spreading to the city. As the Hippodrome was a place where the crowds met the emperor, it was also an ideal setting for public confrontations.[112] The Hippodrome could also be a place where the people showed their support. In 439, Emperor Theodosius II appointed a person named Cyrus as *praetorian prefect* and city prefect, which pleased the citizens quite a bit, and one day, to praise the services that Cyrus rendered to the city, they cheered 'Constantine

---

[110] *Chronicle of Theophanes*, 331 (227).
[111] For acclamations for a victory of charioteers, see Porphyrogennetos, *Book of Ceremonies*, 320–3 (book 1, chapter 69).
[112] Cameron, *Mediterranean World*, 173.

founded it, Cyrus restored it' all day long in the Hippodrome. However, Theodosius was infuriated that Cyrus was held in esteem equal to that of Constantine, hence he stripped Cyrus of his wealth and sent him to exile.[113]

The Hippodrome was also the stage for the iconoclast-versus-iconodule struggle. Emperor Constantine V (r. 741–75), who was most radically iconoclastic, had iconodules lashed during races as part of his fight against monasteries; and to humiliate and to belittle the monks in the eyes of the people, he forced them to parade on the Hippodrome grounds hand-in-hand with women. Some were beheaded while others were blinded.[114] In 767, the same emperor put the deposed patriarch Constantine II (754–66) naked on a donkey, facing the back of the beast, and humiliated him by parading him in the Hippodrome during the races.[115]

The Hippodrome served frequently as a venue for public executions. The semi-circular sphendone section at the south end of the Hippodrome came to be associated with such punishments. Some important executions held here made their way into the Byzantine historical sources. During the reign of Emperor Valens (r. 364–78), the *praepositus* Rhodanus was burned at the stake here.[116] In the era of Leo I (r. 457–74), the *praefectus* Menas was accused of evil deeds and questioned in the Hippodrome by the Senate, after which he was dragged on the ground, and later stoned to death.[117] During the reign of Phokas (r. 602–10), when the Greens ventured upon insulting the emperor during the races, the mutilated limbs of the Greens were hung up in the sphendone.[118] During the reign of Leo III (r. 717–41), the *magister* Nicetas Xylinites was executed by beheading.[119] In the era of Theophilos, the *praepositus* Nikephoros and, in the era of Andronikos I Komnenos (r. 1183–5), Mamalos was burnt at the stake in the Hippodrome.[120] In the twelfth century, Anna Komnena (1083–153), the daughter of Emperor Alexios I Komnenos (r. 1081–118), describes in detail an execution carried out in the Hippodrome. She reports that the monk Basil, leader of the Bogomils, which she considered to be a heretical movement, did not renounce his beliefs despite all efforts of the emperor and was sentenced to death by the Church. The emperor ordered an immense pyre in the Hippodrome. A massive pit was excavated, and mountains of wood were piled in it. As the

---

[113] *Chronicon Paschale*, 78 (450).
[114] Ibid., 605 (437); Treadgold, *History of Byzantine State*, 364–5.
[115] *Chronicle of Theophanes*, 609–10 (441–2).
[116] *Chronicon Paschale*, 47 (369); Guilland, 'Hippodrome', 676–82, see also 881.
[117] *Chronicon Paschale*, 86–7 (465).
[118] *Chronicle of Theophanes* 426 (279); Guilland, 'Hippodrome', 881.
[119] *Patria*, 219 (III, 195).
[120] *Annals of Choniates*, 172 (311, IV, book 1). For executions here, see Guilland, 'Hippodrome', 681–2.

wood was set on fire, a large crowd gathered in the Hippodrome. The fire was so huge that its sparks reached the top of the obelisk. A cross was erected across from the fire, and Basil was asked to choose between the fire and the cross. Basil, who seemed to freeze for a long while, finally decided that angels would come to his rescue and did not renounce on his faith. He was thrown in the fire.[121]

6 Circus Factions and Chariot Races

The most important event held in the Hippodrome was chariot racing. Two-wheeled chariots drawn by four horses competed on the racetrack of the Hippodrome and completed the race by taking seven laps around the spina that divided the track into two. These races and the entertainment held in the Hippodrome were arranged by organised structures known as circus factions.

6.1 Circus Factions

The origin of the Byzantine-era parties organising the chariot races and racing in the Hippodrome goes back to the Romans. The word faction derives from *factio,* which means 'party' in Latin. The equivalent Greek word used for factions is *demus.* During the Roman era, circus factions were independent enterprises with their own stables and horses, chariots, and racers. By contrast, in the Byzantine Empire, they became state-funded structures and hence, to a certain degree, state-controlled. This situation was not only because the emperor was covering the expenses of the chariot races but also because the factions were increasingly becoming part of the official ceremonies of the empire. These organised structures had a leader with the title *factionarius,* who was probably a former charioteer. During the early Byzantine era, this title was given to the most important racers, whereas in the middle Byzantine era, it was only given to the most prominent racers of the Blues and Greens.[122]

In the beginning, just as it was in Rome, four circus factions competed in the races: the Blues, the Greens, the Whites, and the Reds. According to some sources, these four colours represented the basic elements of earth, fire, sea, and air, while others said that they represented the four seasons.[123] Parties (*deme/ demoi*) represented by these colours had their horses, chariots, stables, and charioteers and they organised the races and the entertainments in the Hippodrome. In Constantinople, the Reds and Whites eventually fell behind

---

[121] Anna Komnena, *Anne Comnene: Alexiade*, three vols. Edited and translated Bernard Leib (Paris: Bude, 1937–45), vol. 3, 218–19, 226–7.

[122] Cameron, *Circus Factions*, 11–12.

[123] See Dagron, *L'hippodrome de Constantinople*, 14, 63.

and lost power, while the Blues and Greens continued to exist throughout Byzantine history as powerful supporter organisations. The real competition in the chariot races took place between these two parties. The supporters of these sat side by side, right across the imperial box, in areas reserved for them in the west bleachers, and they cheered for their teams. These parties also had professional cheerleaders to excite the supporters.

These teams were organised somewhat like modern football clubs and their supporter groups, yet they went beyond being mere 'racing clubs' and had various social and political functions. They had three main roles: they organised the chariot races and the Hippodrome entertainments; they were part of the imperial ceremonies; and when the city faced a sudden danger, they functioned as urban militia. When the city was under siege, they helped with the defence, repaired the city walls and other public buildings, and took part in construction activities. One of the most important construction efforts of the circus factions was their work during the building of the city walls under the reign of Theodosius II. Eight thousand men from each party worked on the construction of the walls; the Blues led by Magdalas worked from the coast of the Golden Horn, while the Greens lead by Charisios worked from the coast of the Marmara Sea.[124] During the Avar attack of 583, the factions deployed their men on the Anastasian Wall (the Long Walls of Thrace), 65 kilometres to the west of the city. However, because faction members were not professional soldiers, it is doubtful whether they were effective in serious military operations.[125] These parties were especially powerful and effective in the fifth and sixth centuries. This meant that they would also be the leaders and act as voices of popular disturbance; they were the means to communicate the satisfaction or the dissatisfaction of the people directly to the emperor during the races.

The supporters of these parties were similar to present-day football fans. Fanatic supporters aggressively screamed out slogans in support of their team, wore the colours of their team, and waved the flags of their team. They cheered not only for their team but also for the emperor. Sometimes, the supporters acted as gangs and caused disturbances in the city. In his *Secret History,* Procopius criticises these parties and their supporters. He describes them as individuals with idiosyncratic, Hunnish hairstyles and weird clothing, who cared about nothing but the victory of their own colours, who had no respect for anything holy and no respect for the law.[126] The rivalry of the Greens and Blues sometimes lead to bloody conflicts. Fights among party supporters started in the Hippodrome, and from time to time they spread to the city with serious

---

[124] *Patria*, 91 (II, 58). [125] Cameron, *Circus Factions*, 107–8.
[126] Procopius, *Secret History*, 136–7 (1–6) and for their clothing, see 32–3 (7.8–14).

consequences. In 561, right before the start of the races, a fight broke out between the Blues and the Greens. Emperor Justinian heard this and immediately went up onto the *kathisma* and ordered the chief of the palace guards (*comes excubitorum*) Marinus to intervene; however, Marinus failed to break up the fight, and the Blues invaded the bleachers of the Greens, who responded by stepping out from the Hippodrome into the Mese Avenue, and then occupying and looting the neighbourhoods of the Blues. According to Malalas hundreds of lives were lost during these events.[127]

These parties, especially the Greens and the Blues were also politically active and, controlling large supporter groups, could put pressure on the emperor and therefore muster political leverage. As an example, in 532, in order to appease the unrest that started in the Hippodrome, Emperor Justinian asked them what they wanted. The crowds demanded that the *praetorian prefect* John the Cappadocian, the legal counsel (*quaestor*) Rufinus, and the city prefect Eudaemon be removed from their posts, and the emperor complied.[128] However, this concession did not prevent the uprising from growing and turning into the Nika Revolt, which was the largest in the history of Constantinople. Another illustration of the political activity of these parties can be seen in the appointment of an individual called Plato as city prefect. To appease an uprising that started in the Hippodrome, Emperor Anastasius appointed Plato, the boss of the Greens, to one of the most important and powerful titles in Constantinople.[129]

These parties which were initially independent organisations and which frequently created problems for the emperor, eventually became structures under the control of the monarch. Starting from the seventh century, these parties slowly merged into the palace ceremonies, and the leaders of both parties (*demarchoi*) attained relatively high positions in the palace hierarchy, earning respect and wealth. According to Porphyrogennetos, in the tenth century, the Blues and Greens were to a large extent connected to the palace, and their leaders were appointed as the commanders of the palace's regiment of guards. They were integrated into the ceremonies of the imperial palace, and thus brought under control. Hence, the tendency of the factions to use violence and to terrorise the city was appeased; they were integrated into formal imperial ceremonies held in the Hippodrome, took on important roles as participants and, in a sense, they were 'domesticated'.[130] Again, as far as it can be gathered from

---

[127] *Chronicle of Malalas*, 299 (book 18, 132); also see *Chronicle of Theophanes*, 347 (236).

[128] *Chronicon Paschale*, 116 (530). The text mistakenly names Rufinus as the *quaestor* instead of Tribonian (for Tribonian, see W. E. Kaegi and A. Kazhdan, 'Tribonian'. In *The Oxford Dictionary of Byzantium*, edited by A. Kahzdan and Timothy E. Gregory, 2114 (New York and Oxford: Oxford University Press, 1991).

[129] *Chronicle of Malalas*, 222 (book 16, 4).   [130] Cameron, *Circus Factions*, 27.

The Book of Ceremonies, the race calendar in the Hippodrome took on a religious quality, and it came to be scheduled according to Easter.

The Blue and Green parties were not only organised in the capital Constantinople. They were 'nationwide' organisations that were active in all important cities throughout the entire empire. To give an example, when the consul Damianos, the leader of the Blues in Tarsus, was killed, the Blues in Constantinople rebelled.[131]

The emperors could sometimes be the supporters of one of these parties.[132] For emperors and imperial candidates, it was important to secure the support of the Hippodrome parties, or at least of one party, as well as that of the army. The emperors' support of a circus faction was based on mutual benefit: they would gain the support of a powerful party, and the party benefitted from their power. Emperor Arcadius was a fan of the Greens. He stated, 'I want to see the Greens right in front of me' and he had the Blues removed from the Hippodrome bleachers that faced the imperial box and got the Greens to sit there, giving them ample room.[133] Theodosius II also supported the Greens.[134] Emperor Anastasius got angry with the Greens and the Blues for starting uprisings in many cities of the empire, and he started supporting the party of the Reds in Constantinople.[135] Emperor Justinian was a supporter of the Blue faction.[136] After Justinian's death, before the races held in 568, as the supporters of the Blues and Greens got in a fight in the Hippodrome, Emperor Justin II (r. 565–78) turned to the Greens and stated 'Emperor Justinian is dead, he is no longer amongst you', and he turned to the Blues and stated 'Emperor Justinian is dead, but he still lives amongst you' and managed to diffuse the situation.[137] Emperor Marcian (r. 450–7) was an adherent of the Blues. After an uprising organised by the Greens, he banned them from all official and administrative duties for three years.[138]

As the imperial palace, which was adjacent to the Hippodrome, was gradually moved to the new palace in the Blachernai area (present-day Ayvansaray), located in the north-west end of the city, in the twelfth century, the connection between the palace and the Hippodrome was severed to a great extent, and as a result of a decrease in imperial ceremonies held in the Hippodrome, the role of circus factions diminished, and they eventually vanished.[139]

---

[131] Procopius, *Secret History*, 128 (32–3).
[132] See Dagron, *L'hippodrome de Constantinople*, 208–11.
[133] *Chronicle of Malalas*, 191 (book 14, 2).   [134] Cameron, *Porphyrius*, 228.
[135] *Chronicle of Malalas*, 220 (book 16, 2).
[136] Ibid., 245 (book 18, 1); Procopius, *Secret History*, 32 (7.1).
[137] *Chronicle of Theophanes*, 358 (243).   [138] *Chronicle of Malalas*, 202 (book 14, 34).
[139] Cameron, *Circus Factions*, 308.

6.2 Chariot Races

In the Hippodrome of Constantinople, races gained immense popularity, start-ing in the fourth century and continued intensely until the late sixth century. By the tenth century, the 'ancient' characteristics of Hippodrome races had changed to a great extent. The role of the emperor in the races increased, and imperial ceremonies gained prominence; the calendar of the races was Christianised and made compatible with the liturgical calendar. The races became increasingly rare in the Middle Ages and were only held on special occasions. Yet, there were two significant races with dates that did not change: the race held on 11 May to commemorate the anniversary of the founding of Constantinople[140] and the Devotion Day race held on 1 January. Theophanes states that on 11 May 712/713, 'the birthday of the city' was celebrated with chariot races, in which the party of the Greens emerged victorious.[141] In addition, chariot races were also held on the occasion of events involving the imperial family such as coron-ations, marriage ceremonies, and birthdays. During the fourth and fifth centur-ies, approximately sixty-six races were held every year in the Hippodrome of Constantinople, but in the tenth century this fell to twelve. Compared to the early era, the number of races held on the same day decreased to a total of eight races: four took place before noon and four after.[142]

Races were essentially organised by circus factions. During the early Byzantine period, these parties had their own race chariots, horses, stables, and racers. But later, because of the high expense associated with chariot races, the emperor funded them, and the imperial stables and horses came to be used for this purpose. The continuous maintenance that the Hippodrome needed, acquiring and maintaining the best horses and chariots, and organising spec-tacular ceremonies, all required a massive team. At the top of this hierarchy was a master of ceremonies responsible for the organisation of the races. In addition, each party had grooms caring for the horses, and charioteers had assistants helping them, as well as physicians, security guards and many professionals who performed between the races. There were many officials who ensured order in the Hippodrome before and during the races.[143] These individuals accom-plished many tasks such as maintaining the racetrack, arranging the layout of the benches, removing wrecked chariots from the racetrack, and counting the laps.

---

[140] This race is described in detail in Porphyrogennetos, *Book of Ceremonies*, 340–8 (book 1, chapter 70).

[141] *Chronicle of Theophanes*, 533 (381).

[142] Charlotte Roueché, 'Partiler ve Eğlenceler/The Factions and Entertainment', in *Hippodrom/Atmeydanı*, vol. 1, 52–3.

[143] Dagron, *L'hippodrome de Constantinople*, 109–15.

The races would last almost all day, and between the races, various types of entertainment with music, dancing, and acrobatics, featuring various exotic animals, were offered for the pleasure of the spectators.[144] However, unlike in Rome, the Hippodrome of Constantinople featured no gladiatorial fights, and no pantomimes, which was considered a pagan Greek tradition. In 498, Emperor Anastasius banned fighting, hunting, and killing wild beasts (*venationes*) in the Hippodrome, and gradually pantomime shows were prohibited in all cities. The Church was also against these shows. Of course, the extreme cost of acquiring wild beasts such as lions and tigers also contributed to this ban. However, the interest of Byzantine citizens in wild and exotic animals never waned. The animals would be paraded in the Hippodrome in front of excited spectators – hence the custom of exhibiting wild beasts continued without the shedding of blood.[145] These shows were also carried out by the factions. The Blues and the Greens had dancing masters in charge of the entertainment, who held important positions in the hierarchy of the faction. Wild beasts who took part in the Hippodrome shows also had caretakers. According to Procopius, the father of Empress Theodora, Akakios took care of the Green party's beasts, and he was known as the 'keeper of the bears'.[146] Procopius also mentions a dancing master named Asterios who was probably a high-ranking official responsible for arranging the dancing and the entertainment shows.[147]

Although there were twelve starting gates, for the most part, four – and sometimes eight – were used if one chariot per team was to race. The chariots started the race from the western track and completed the race by taking seven counterclockwise laps around the spina. The finish line was in the section in front of the bleachers on the west side reserved for the supporters of the Blue and Green parties. Chariots of all four parties participated in the race; however, two of these, the Blues and the Greens, were prominent. The Reds were to a certain extent under the control of the Blues, while the Whites were under the Greens. So, the Reds and the Whites were to a large extent affiliated with them. If more than one racer from each team competed, a team member could resort to various strategies so that a more advantageous individual from his own team could win; he would try to constrain the rival charioteers so that they would fall behind.

The patron of the chariot races was the emperor himself, and it was his privilege to start the races. Accompanied by the patricians and the *strategoi*, the emperor would come from the palace to the *kathisma* and would stand in front of his throne to greet the people in the Hippodrome by crossing them. Then, he would sit on the throne and start the races.[148] The emperor and the

---

[144] Mango, 'History of Hippodrome', 40.   [145] Cameron, *Porphyrius*, 231.
[146] Procopius, *Secret History*, 40 (9.2–7), n. 37.   [147] Ibid. (9.5).
[148] Porphyrogennetos, *Book of Ceremonies*, 307 (book 1, chapter 68, V.71).

public face each other at the Hippodrome, but this is a visual communication rather than verbal; he addressed the public indirectly through the *mandator*.[149]

The Hippodrome was not solely dedicated to chariot races. It was occupied by crowds throughout most of the day to watch various performances such as displays of literary skills or rhetoric, acrobatics, dance, and music. The Hippodrome also had pipe organs that belonged to the Blues and Greens. In the relief located in the south-east base of the Egyptian obelisk, one organ is seen at either end of the lower row where the musicians and dancers are depicted. One aspect of the Hippodrome was that it was the liveliest public space of the city, where citizens could meet, watch these shows, and chat.

6.2.1 The Hoisting of the Flag

Races were announced to the city through a large flag known as *velum* that was hoisted in the Hippodrome upon the order of the emperor. Once the flag was hoisted, if races were to be postponed due to a storm or similar reason, it would remain up until the day of the races. If the flag was brought down, this indicated that the races were cancelled, not postponed.[150] The hoisting of a flag in the Hippodrome by the emperor meant that chariot races would start.[151] When Zeno became emperor in 476, his first act was to organise chariot races in the Hippodrome, and he hoisted the flag.[152] In case of an emergency such as a fire, a siege, or the like, the emperor would also hoist a flag to gather people into the Hippodrome. During the Nika Revolt, Emperor Justinian had a flag hoisted on the Hippodrome.[153] According to *The Book of Ceremonies*, when a prince was born in the purple room, the emperor would order a flag to be hoisted in the Hippodrome and would announce this blessed event to the people by organising chariot races. There is no information about how the flag was raised, or where in the Hippodrome the flag mast was located.

6.2.2 Drawing of Lots

The line-up of party chariots in the race was determined by drawing lots. This process was taken extremely seriously and involved a lengthy and complex ritual. Basically, balls belonging to each party were placed inside a large lot-casting urn and removed while it was still being turned. *The Book of Ceremonies* describes in detail a drawing of lots from the tenth century. Representatives of the Blues and the Greens also attended the long ceremonial

---

[149] Dagron, *L'hippodrome de Constantinople*, 230–4.
[150] Porphyrogennetos, *Book of Ceremonies*, 339 (book 1, chapter 69).
[151] Ibid., 364 (book 1, chapter 73), 617 (book 2, chapter 21); Guilland, 'Hippodrome', 677.
[152] *Chronicle of Malalas*, 210 (book 15, 5).   [153] Ibid., 275–6 (book 18, 474).

drawing. The urn would be positioned in the middle of the tribunal, and the representatives of the Blues and Greens would place two balls bearing their own party's colours inside the urn. On either side of the urn would be the factional representatives, behind these were the two programme writers who prepared the programme of the races, and still behind them stood high-level functionaries. The chariot racers sat on the sides of the urn. One overseer would start spinning the urn and the balls would be thrown inside. The urn would be turned three times. The charioteers and their racing order would be determined according to the balls that fell, or that were removed from the urn. The imperial programme writers recorded these results and prepared the race programmes accordingly.[154] Since the inner lane of the racetrack was the most advantageous, the first winner of the draw got to compete here, the later draws would line up from the inner lanes to the outer ones.

6.2.3 Charioteers

Prominent charioteers gained great popularity, statues of some were erected during their lifetime, and epigrams were written for them. Of the many epigrams written for Libyan-born Porphyrius, the most famous of these charioteers, thirty-two have survived until today.[155] Some of these epigrams are in the form of short texts on sculpture bases, as mentioned previously regarding the base of Porphyrius' sculpture. The statues of the charioteers stood in the Hippodrome, possibly on the spina. In addition to Porphyrius, there were other famous charioteers whose names survived and whose statues are known to exist, such as Ouranicus, Faustinus, Julian, and Constantine.[156]

Some charioteers who were famed across the empire competed in races in other cities. For example, in addition to Constantinople, Porphyrius also competed in Nicomedia as well as in Antioch.[157] The famous charioteer, who was also known as Kalliopas, went from Constantinople to Antioch and won great victories here as a racer of the Green faction.[158]

Famous charioteers could compete for Greens sometimes, and for Blues at other times. For example, Porphyrius raced on behalf of both teams. One of the two sculpture bases belonging to Porphyrius exhibited in the Istanbul Archaeological Museums was built by the Greens, and the other by the Blues. There are at least seven statues known to belong to Porphyrius, four built by the Blues, and the other three by Greens.[159] Emperor Anastasius encouraged Porphyrius to compete for both

---

[154] Porphyrogennetos, *Book of Ceremonies*, 312–13 (book 1, chapter 69).

[155] Cameron, *Mediterranean World*, 173.   [156] Bardill, 'Monuments', 178.

[157] Mango, 'History of Hippodrome', 40.   [158] *Chronicle of Malalas*, 222 (book 16, 6).

[159] Bardill, 'Monuments', 177.

the Blues and the Greens, and hence aimed to make it possible for supporters of both parties to savour victory, which was a measure taken to prevent the build-up of tension. This was a means to satisfy supporters of both parties.

Charioteers would wear the colours of the team that they competed for. They usually had a long-sleeved shirt that fully covered the body with a sleeveless, embroidered tunic on top. At waist-level, there was a tight, wide belt. For good luck, they would wear around their necks a type of amulet known as a *bulla*. Their legs were covered with a kind of cross-gartering like modern puttees. Charioteers would not be allowed to compete without a helmet on. A charioteer who dropped his helmet during the race would be disqualified even if he reached the finish line. If a charioteer could knock the helmet off another charioteer, he would be considered to have won the race in first place no matter in what sequence he finished it.

An anonymous epigram refers to the images of the four famous charioteers located on the ceiling of the imperial box of the Hippodrome and praises them. According to Mango's interpretation, these belonged to the end of the fifth or to the beginning of the sixth century. This epigram depicts Porphyrius, the charioteer for the Blues, then states:

> '[he] has been nobly carried up to race even in the air. This man, who has vanquished all the chariot-drivers of the World, mounts up that he may race with the Sun.' For the charioteer of the Greens, 'Faustinus, the former glory of the Greens, would have risen to heaven, racing his horses as if he were alive.' For the charioteer of the Whites, 'This was Constantine who in olden times drove with agility the quadriga of the White colour.' For Julian, the charioteer of the Reds, 'this charioteer would have been ready once again to take the lead and win the crown'.[160]

In order to reveal the true skills of the individual who competed, the horses would be exchanged after the first race, and a new race would be held. The four horses that the Blues raced with would be given to the Greens, and vice versa. This horse exchange, called the *diversium*, was dependent on the desire and the authorisation of the emperor. A charioteer who won the race with both sets of horses proved that the skill was with the rider and not the horses. The *diversium* was observed only during the Byzantine era and did not exist in the Roman-era races. This exchange is depicted on the famous Porphyrius statue base: an individual is seen holding in one hand the reins of four horses standing on the right side, and in his other, those of four horses standing on the other side (see Figure 13, lower panel).

The racers would complete the race by taking seven laps around the spina. In front of the emperor sitting in his imperial box, the charioteer who won the race

---

[160] Translated from Anthologia Graeca by Cyril Mango, *The Art of the Byzantine Empire, 312–1453: Sources and Documents* (Toronto: Toronto University Press, 1986), 49–50.

would receive the wreath from the hand of the emperor's herald. At this point, the charioteer would be standing in front of the emperor without his helmet and whip. The victorious charioteer would be crowned and given a palm branch (*baion*). In addition, a measure (*modios*) full of coins was given as an award. The spectators would cheer both for the charioteer and for the emperor. Regardless of the colour of the winning racer, the victory was believed to come from God, and ultimately was attributed to the emperor.[161]

Chariot races were quite competitive and hence could get quite dangerous. Malalas reports that during a race in 363, a racer called Julianicus fell, was dragged around the Hippodrome, and died.[162]

There is no doubt that the most famous of the chariot racers was Porphyrius, who had multiple statues erected while he was still alive.[163] Using the surviving thirty-two epigrams written in the Greek anthology for Porphyrius, Aleksandr A. Vasiliev produced a brief biography (*vita*) of the famous charioteer. According to this, Porphyrius, son of Calchas, was of African origin, and was brought to Constantinople from Alexandria at a young age.[164] Some sources state that the charioteer, who was also known as Kalliopas, started his career in the Blue faction; however, later he attracted the attention of Emperor Anastasius who was a Green-faction supporter and started racing for the Greens upon the monarch's request. The height of his career coincides with the reign of Anastasius between 491 and 518. He became famous at a very young age, and with the permission of the emperor, his bronze statue was erected in the Hippodrome. An exaggerated epigram stated that 'his statue must not be bronze like that of the others, but gold'. Another epigram compared him to Alexander the Great. In 507, Porphyrius arrived at Antioch and 'he took over the stable of the Green faction, which was vacant, and was completely victorious'.[165] After a while, he participated in the Olympic games held in Daphne. Meanwhile, under his leadership, the Antiochians attacked and plundered the Daphne synagogue, and killed a lot of people.[166] When he was over sixty, he continued to compete. During the era of Emperor Justin I (r. 518–27), he again competed on behalf of the Blues because the emperor supported the Blues. Because he competed and won great victories for both factions, he was

---

[161] Dagron, *L'hippodrome de Constantinople*, 241–2.

[162] *Chronicle of Malalas*, 304 (book 18, 144).

[163] This is defined by the inscription on the pedestal of the sculpture of Porphyrius now on exhibition at the Istanbul Archaeological Museums. For the translation of the inscription, see earlier.

[164] Vasiliev, 'Monument of Porphyrius', 40–8.

[165] *Chronicle of Malalas*, 222 (book 16, 395–6).

[166] Dagron, *L'hippodrome de Constantinople*, 312.

beloved by fans of either side, and his statues appeared in the spaces in the Hippodrome belonging to both parties.

6.2.4 Race Chariots and Horses

The chariots competing in the Hippodrome were drawn by four horses, had two wheels, and the charioteer would ride them standing up. These were extremely fast and highly manoeuvrable war chariots.

Just like their charioteers, some horses that won victories in the Hippodrome were famous by name. Foals from many parts of the empire were carefully selected for competition. Cappadocia was known as 'the land of beautiful horses'. Grooms and veterinarians cared for the horses acquired, they were trained, kept healthy, and were worked constantly so that they remained in form. Sometimes, a fortune was paid for a good horse. On the pedestal of the Porphyrius sculpture, the names of the horses were also indicated. During the early Byzantine period, the horses belonged to the circus factions which were independent organisations, later, especially after the seventh century, horses were procured from the imperial stables.

Constantine Porphyrogennetos relates how horses were adorned and paraded in front of the emperor during chariot races held on the anniversary of Constantinople's foundation: both parties brought out their horses wearing saddle-clothing edged with gold bands, collars, and bridles.[167] While cheering to the emperor, faction members paraded the horses all the way to the sphendone.

As long as the horses could race, their tails would remain tied; however, as they got so old that they could not compete or when they got hurt, their tails would be untied. An untied horse tail indicated that its racing career had come to an end.

Rules governed how a horse could be changed if it fell ill or could no longer compete. One instructor from each of the factions, and two overseers and a superintendent examined the horse carefully and, if they concluded that it could not compete, they replaced it with another. If the incapacitated horse was scheduled for the first race, they replaced it with a horse from the third; however, this horse would still compete in the third race.[168] If a horse fell during the races, the representatives of two parties went to check, and if the horse could race again it was taken to the stables (*diippion*) to be cared for while its tail was still tied.[169] But if they believed that the horse was done for, they untied its tail, and they removed the horse by dragging it from the feet.

---

[167] Porphyrogennetos, *Book of Ceremonies*, 341 (book 1, chapter 70).
[168] Ibid., 333 (book 1, chapter 69).   [169] Ibid., 339–40 (book 1, chapter 69).

7 The Church's Opposition to the Chariot Races

The Church never saw chariot races in a positive light, and never approved of them. Participants in the races were heavily criticised in the sermons of religious figures of the early Christian age, such as St John Chrysostom (349–407), or in their *vitae*. Yet, these races were so deeply rooted in the strong Roman imperial tradition that the Church never succeeded in reducing the interest of the populace in hippodrome activities, and never managed to ban the races. Despite its initial rejection of hippodrome activities and chariot races, the Church eventually accepted them. Emperors supported hippodrome activities and ensured their continuation because they were integral parts of the cult of the emperor and imperial ceremonies. As circus factions were integrated into imperial ceremonies and received the support of the empire, the Church reluctantly acknowledged their existence and, to a certain extent, even took part in these Hippodrome ceremonies. The patriarch also attended the festival known as 'Hippodrome of Vegetables', organised to mark the anniversary of the foundation of Constantinople which also featured chariot races. During this festival, bread, fish, and especially vegetables were distributed to the poor free of charge, and the Church took credit for this display of charity.

The position of the Church against the activities in the Hippodrome can be illustrated with three examples from various periods. The first example comes from the late antique era, which witnessed the epitome of hippodrome entertainment and chariot races. In his sermons, St John Chrysostom, who was the patriarch of Constantinople from 398 to 404, criticised the chariot races and equated them to 'submission to the devil'. According to the patriarch, the participants were wasting their time, were nullifying the education the Church provided them, and the hippodrome races had almost become a substitute for religion. In his account of the Parable of Lazarus and the Rich Man, he states:

> some of those who listen to this [sermon] have forgotten everything and surrendered themselves again to the satanic spectacle of the races ... They give greater applause to the charioteers and show an uncontrollable frenzy. They rush together with great excitement and often wrangle with one another, saying that one horse ran badly, another was tripped and fell. One person attaches himself to one charioteer, another to the other. They have no thought or memory of our words, nor of the spiritual and awesome mysteries which are celebrated here; but like captives in the snares of the devil, they spend the whole day there, surrendering themselves to the satanic spectacle.[170]

---

[170] St. John Chrysostom. *On Wealth and Poverty*, translated by Catharine P. Roth (Crestwood, NY: St. Vladimir's Seminary Press, 1984), 125–6.

Another example is from St Stephen's (713–64) biography. The *vita* of the saint refers to the iconoclastic Emperor Constantine V as a tyrant, and it criticises the removal from the Mese of the images of six holy men, and their replacement with the image of a chariot racer. The images originally were commissioned by the previous pious emperors to explain the Orthodox faith to the people of the city and to outsiders: 'a satanic horse-race and that demon-loving charioteer . . . called Ouranikos . . . he who was unworthy both of heaven and earth, [and] he honoured him more than he did the holy Fathers [of the Church]'.[171]

Alice-Mary Talbot relates another example of Christianity's opposition to hippodrome shows, from the biography of St Basil the Younger. The land-owner Gregorios, a disciple of this holy man who passed away in 944 in Constantinople, stepped out of his house one day, and headed for the saint's lodge, when he happened to pass by the Hippodrome he noted that races were about to begin. For quite some time, he struggled with himself, because the saint he was devoted to did not approve of spending time in the Hippodrome. Eventually, he caved in and entered the Hippodrome to watch the first race. As he reached the lodge, the holy man already knew that he had watched the races and scolded him. He accused Gregorios of 'throwing himself before the demon of the chariot races' which were 'invented by [the demons] long ago for the destruction of human souls' and complained that these races were still continued.[172] Although it is a polemical source, this example gives us an idea of the attitude of Christianity towards the Hippodrome races in the tenth century, but is also quite interesting in that it demonstrates how much of a great passion these races continued to be for the inhabitants of Constantinople.

As they criticised the activities in the Hippodrome, the Christian clergy were probably exaggerating. They believed that Hippodrome activities involved pagan elements, nude shows, pagan statues, dancing, prostitution, violence, and atrocities. It is true that the early ages of Byzantine hippodrome festivals featured pagan elements, eroticism, and violence; however, towards the Middle Ages, bloody gladiator fights, hunting wild animals, and pantomime shows with pagan elements were banned, and imperial ceremonies gained prominence. Even so, sculptures of which the Church disapproved, chariot races which were considered a waste of time, and entertainments in the Hippodrome all continued to exist in one form or another throughout the history of Constantinople. Despite all the power it exerted, the Church was unable to

[171] Translated from *Vita Stephani* by Mango, *Art of the Byzantine Empire*, 153.
[172] Alice-Mary Talbot, 'Orta Bizans Döneminde Hippodrom'un Cazibesi/The Lure of the Hippodrome in the Middle Byzantine Era', in *Hippodrom/Atmeydanı*, vol. 1, 65–8, see 66.

bring an end to the hippodrome activities that were integral for imperial ceremonies. The real concern of the clergy was that the hippodrome activities alienated their congregation from the Church, and perhaps that money that was potentially Church revenue was being wasted in the Hippodrome.

8 The Hippodrome During the Ottoman Period

Although most of the architectural elements of the Hippodrome disappeared completely during the Ottoman period, the spacious area where races were held was kept intact and continued to serve as a venue for more or less similar functions. Following the Ottoman conquest, this area was not made available for construction, and despite the construction of many very large structures such as the Ibrahim Pasha Palace and Sultanahmet Mosque around the Hippodrome, this precious area was consciously left vacant. Spacious squares do not feature much in Ottoman urban design; however, the wide space of the Hippodrome in the heart of the Ottoman Istanbul served as a city square. To a certain extent, the Hippodrome continued its social function in a similar manner: various ceremonial activities of the Sultan and his family, horse races and a game called 'cirit', in which riders on horses throw lances to each other, certain insurgency attempts, and some executions were held here. On certain days a market for the trading of horses took place. Hence, during the Ottoman period the area came to be known as 'Atmeydanı', that is 'the square of the horses'.

Following the seizure of Constantinople by Ottomans in 1453, with the exception of the three monuments on the spina of the Hippodrome, architectural elements such as usable columns and fine stone blocks were taken and re-used in new structures built in the area. In 1521, Sultan Suleiman's (r. 1520–66) Grand Vizier Ibrahim Pasha (1493–536), a *devşirme* (a conscript of Christian origin) from Parga, constructed his palace in the space making up the western side of the bleachers of the Byzantine Hippodrome. During the construction of this palace, which serves today as the Museum of Turkish and Islamic Arts, Ibrahim Pasha removed the west wing of the Hippodrome completely and reused its stones. Judging from the position of the palace and sphendone section, the section below the Ibrahim Pasha Palace should be the western benches of the Hippodrome. During restoration efforts in the Museum, the removal of a boiler in the second courtyard of the palace revealed vaulted tunnels belonging to the infrastructure of the Hippodrome's benches. These ruins are aligned in the same direction as similar infrastructural elements in the north and south which were revealed during previous excavations and outside of the palace structure, hence they point to the location of the benches on the western side of the Hippodrome. In the present day, these ruins are exhibited within the museum in situ.[173] The Sultanahmet Mosque was built in 1609, on the eastern side of the Hippodrome where the bleachers and the adjacent Byzantine imperial palace area were, and the bleachers and the imperial box were completely removed. During the construction, the rubble removed from the foundation pits of the Ibrahim Pasha Palace and the Sultanahmet Mosque was spread on the Hippodrome area, and the racetrack was buried approximately 5 metres below the level of the present-day promenade.[174] A look at the pedestals of the three monuments which have survived on the spina reveals this situation today.

It is fortunate that the three large monuments on the spina, the Egyptian obelisk, the Serpent column, and the Walled obelisk, have survived until the present day. During the Ottoman period, these monuments, and especially the Serpent column, were perceived as talismans protecting the city against various evils and were not destroyed. The renowned Ottoman traveller Evliya Çelebi (1611–82) mentions in his *Seyahatname* many talismans protecting the city of Istanbul, including the three monuments in the Hippodrome. The accounts and the drawings of fifteenth-century travellers reveal which sections of the Hippodrome were still standing at that time. Among these, the most detailed and accurate information comes from Onofrio Panvinio's (1529–68) sixteenth-century carving. The carved map of Constantinople produced by Buondelmonti (1386–c.1430), who visited the city in the 1420s, depicts the Hippodrome and some of its artwork; however, Buondelmonti's drawings are not very realistic in terms of the structures and their positions within the topography of the Hippodrome. A sixteenth-century Ottoman miniature by Nasûhü's Silâhi (known as Matrakçı Nasuh) clearly depicts the situation of the Hippodrome during the period of Suleiman the Magnificent (Figure 16).[175] This miniature shows the three monuments in the spina of the Hippodrome: the Egyptian obelisk, the Serpent column with its three snakes, and the Walled obelisk. In addition, along the spina, to the north of the Egyptian obelisk and to the south of the Walled obelisk, two monumental columns can be seen. The semi-circular sphendone section of the Hippodrome has been depicted along with the eight columns on it. On top of the columns, the architrave is still standing. The miniature features the palace of Ibrahim Pasha in the foreground, while many

[173] For these remains, see Akyürek, 'Konstantinopolis Hipodromu', 144–9.
[174] Müller-Wiener, *Bildlexikon*, 69.
[175] Nasûhü's Silâhi. *Beyan-ı Menâzil-i Sefer-i Irâkeyn-i Sultân Süleymân Hân* (Istanbul: Rare Masterpieces Department of Istanbul University Library), T 5964, fol. 8b 9a; Also see Nurhan Atasoy, *Silahşor, Tarihçi, Matematikçi, Nakkaş, Hattat: Matrakçı Nasuh ve Menzilnamesi* (Istanbul: Masa, 2015), 38 fig. 8b, 43 fig. 8b/12.

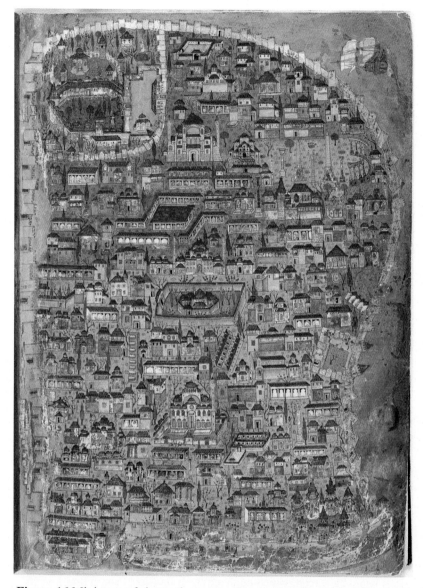

Figure 16 Miniature of sixteenth-century Constantinople, *Beyân-ı Menâzil-i Sefer-i Irâkeyn-i Sultân Süleymân Hân*, Rare Masterpieces Department of Istanbul University Library, T 5964, detail from 9a 9b

structures in the eastern side of the Hippodrome can be seen, as the Sultanahmet Mosque has not yet been constructed. Some of the large columns on the sphendone may have been recycled and reused in the construction of the Sultanahmet Mosque.

During the Ottoman period, the wide flat of the racetrack of the Hippodrome was largely preserved as one of the widest squares of the city, and continued serving as a venue for various entertainments and ceremonies. Celebrations of weddings and circumcisions of the sultan's family, festivals, and various ceremonies – albeit not so frequently as under the Byzantine emperors – were held here. The first ceremony on record was the celebration of the circumcision of Sultan Bayezid II's (r. 1481–512) son in 1490, which lasted for days. Two week long celebrations marking the marriage of Sultan Suleiman's sister Hatice Sultan to Ibrahim Pasha were also held here in 1524. These types of festivities continued until the seventeenth century, and the last known ceremony was held in 1646 on the occasion of the marriage of Fatma Sultan, who was Sultan Ibrahim the Fool's sister. However, the most magnificent and well-documented ceremony to be held in the Hippodrome area was in 1582, on the occasion of the circumcision of Mehmed III, Sultan Murad III's (r. 1574–95) son. It featured ceremonies and festivities lasted fifty-two days. All inhabitants of Istanbul were invited to these festivities and people were given feasts, and various entertainments and shows were organised. It was interesting that musicians and acrobats, as well as all professional groups and artisan guilds of the city, were represented during the pageant, each one displaying their skills and their products. While architects participated with a large-scale model of the Süleymaniye Mosque, candy makers walked with large, sweet animal figures. The celebrations of the circumcision of Prince Mehmed III have been depicted in 427 miniatures in Nakkaş Osman's manuscript dating from 1582.[176]

Another purpose of these ceremonies was to display the power of the sultan and the empire to the people and to the whole world. In addition to the people of Istanbul, foreign ambassadors, and on occasion, other sovereigns were invited to these ceremonies. The sultans would watch these ceremonies from a balcony in the Ibrahim Pasha Palace overseeing Atmeydanı, just as the Byzantine emperors watched chariot races from the *kathisma* on the other side. One difference is that, during Hippodrome ceremonies, Byzantine emperors would appear in public directly, while Ottoman sultans watched these ceremonies and festivities behind a screen, which rendered them invisible. Yet, it was known that the sultan was present watching the festivities, and his authority was felt heavily.

Starting from the middle of the seventeenth century, some festivals and ceremonies held in the Hippodrome were moved to the suburbs of the city, onto the wide prairies in districts such as Okmeydanı, Kağıthane, and Beykoz.

---

[176] See Nurhan Atasoy, *Surname-i Humayun: An Imperial Celebration* (Istanbul: Koçbank Yayınları, 1997).

When the Ottoman palace was moved from Topkapı to Dolmabahçe in 1853, Atmeydanı had to a great extent lost its connection to the palace; however, the area continued to be used for various purposes even if not for imperial ceremonies, and occasionally served as military training grounds and as marketplace on some days. In the eighteenth century, Atmeydanı, which had witnessed the *Janissary* and *Sipahi*[177] uprisings, also continued to be the meeting place of the people of the city to celebrate religious days.[178] In 1863, an international fair was organised in this area, and an eye-catching, temporary building was constructed, and in its various pavilions more than 10,000 products and foods brought from many areas of the empire were exhibited. A year later, the fair building was dismantled and removed from the area.[179] In present-day Istanbul, the wide square, which is still called Atmeydanı, hosts various entertainment activities during Islam's holy month of Ramadan.

9 Archaeological Research and Excavations Conducted in the Hippodrome and Vicinity

The Hippodrome attracted the attention of Western archaeologists and historians as early as the nineteenth century, and the first excavations started in the middle of that century, although they were not scientific and systematic.[180] In 1855, Charles Thomas Newton conducted an excavation around the Serpent column, and revealed its pedestal. The next year, soldiers from the British corps of engineers who were brought to Istanbul because of the Crimean war, excavated around the other two obelisks, and revealed the bases of these monuments. In 1918 and 1932, Ernst Mamboury and Theodore Wiegand carried out minor excavation work around the imperial palace and the Hippodrome, attempting to determine the dimensions of the Hippodrome in the south-west and east sections.[181] They made some measurements based on existing remains, and tried to draw a plan of the Hippodrome. In 1927–8, Stanley Casson and David Talbot Rice carried out systematic excavations under the supervision of the Istanbul Archaeological Museums, and they opened trenches around the Walled

---

[177] *Janissary* and *Sipahi* were two different types of Ottoman corps. While *Janissaries*, meaning 'new soldier', were elite infantry units, *Sipahis* were cavalry corps.

[178] Müller-Wiener, *Bildlexikon*, 69.

[179] Nurcan Yazıcı, 'İlk Osmanlı Sergi binası ve Mimar Bourgeois – Parvillée – Montani İşbirliği/ The First Ottoman Exhibition Building in Atmeydanı and the Collaboration of Architects Bourgeois – Parvillée – Montani', in *Hippodrom/Atmeydanı*, vol. 2, 128–51.

[180] For a brief summary of the archaeological works performed at the Hippodrome, see Bardill, 'Archaeologists and Excavations'.

[181] Robert Demangel and Ernest Mamboury, *Le Quartier des Manganes et la première région de Constantinople*. Recherches françaises en Turquie 2 (Paris: Editions de Boccard, 1939).

Figure 17 Substructure of the bleachers revealed after excavations, Archive of
the Istanbul Archaeological Museums

obelisk, the Serpent column, the Egyptian obelisk, and in the western section
where the bleachers once stood.[182]

However, the most comprehensive excavations at the Hippodrome were
carried out by Rüstem Duyuran, the deputy director of the Istanbul
Archaeological Museums in the 1950s, during the construction of the new
courthouse. In excavations carried out on the north side of the Ibrahim Pasha
Palace on the western end of the Hippodrome, many metres of rubble and
some wall remains from the recent era were removed. Excavations carried out
in this section revealed some of the steps belonging to the benches on the
western side of the Hippodrome, in situ. The ruins, which are made up of eight
rows of steps 12 metres long, and the supporting infrastructural walls have

---

[182] Stanley Casson, David Talbot Rice, A. Hugh Martin Jones, and Geoffrey Francis Hudson,
*Preliminary Report upon the Excavations Carried out in the Hippodrome of Constantinople in
1927 on behalf of the British Academy* (London: Oxford University Press, 1928);
Stanley Casson, David Talbot Rice, Basil Gray, and Geoffrey Francis Hudson, *Second Report
upon the Excavations Carried Out in and Near the Hippodrome of Constantinople in 1928 on
behalf of the British Academy* (London: Oxford University Press, 1929).

Figure 18 Steps ascending to the upper benches, Archive of the Istanbul
Archaeological Museums

provided invaluable information concerning the bleachers of the Hippodrome
(Figure 17). A trench opened in front of these benches went 5 metres deep, and
the ground of the Hippodrome and the benches of the front support walls were
revealed. Later, a 1.83 metre-thick portion of the wall about 70 metres in
length that supported the benches has also been unearthed. Behind this wall,
parallel to it, a row of thick piers made of bricks has been found. These piers
were connected to the outer wall of the Hippodrome on the west side. And in
the eastern side of these piers, a vaulted corridor forming the infrastructure of
the benches rising step by step has been found. On the eastern side of this
corridor towards the racetrack, a few steps belonging to the lower sections of
the benches have been spotted. A staircase with marble steps and railing,
ascending to the upper benches, has been unearthed in a well-preserved state
(Figure 18).[183]

---

[183] Rüstem Duyuran, 'İstanbul Adalet Sarayı inşaatı yerinde yapılan kazılar hakkındaki ilk rapor/
First Report on Excavations on the Site of the New Palace of Justice at Istanbul', *İstanbul
Arkeoloji Müzeleri Yıllığı* 5 (1952): 23–32, 33–8.

In 1951, during the second excavation season led by Duyuran, from 11 April to 14 May, a short-duration effort was undertaken in the north-west section of the Hippodrome. During the excavation seasons, a total of forty-six Byzantine coins was found, most being from the ninth and twelfth centuries.[184] In the light of the archaeological data obtained from these Hippodrome excavations, it was possible to make a true restitution of its bleachers.[185]

A marble bench discovered by chance in the courtyard of the Sultanahmet Mosque provides some idea about the shape of the benches on these steps. This marble bench stands today in the courtyard of the mosque, in the section overlooking the Hippodrome. Archaeological excavations to be conducted in the Hippodrome area using new technologies will lead to the unveiling of this greatest architectural structure after the city walls of Byzantine Constantinople. In order to determine the northern boundary of the Hippodrome, these excavation efforts should be carried out in this area. In addition, excavations meant to reveal the racetrack should be carried out between the bleachers and the spina, and excavations to reveal the spina wall should be carried out between the two obelisks.

---

[184] Rüstem Duyuran, 'İstanbul Adalet Sarayı inşaat yerinde yapılan kazılar hakkında ikinci rapor/ Second Report on Excavations on the Site of the New Palace of Justice at Istanbul', *İstanbul Arkeoloji Müzeleri Yıllığı* 6 (1953): 21–7, 74–80.

[185] For a restitution of the bleachers of the Hippodrome, see Bardill, 'Architecture and Archaeology', 124, fig. 8.32.

Bibliography

Primary Sources

Accounts of Medieval Constantinople, The Patria. Translated by Albrecht Berger. London and Cambridge, MA: Harvard University Press, 2013.

Chronicon Paschale, 284–628 A.D. Translated by Michael Whitby and Mary Whitby. Liverpool: Liverpool University Press, 2007.

The Chronicle of John Malalas. Translated by Elizabeth Jeffreys, Michael Jeffreys, and Roger Scott. Melbourne: Australian Association for Byzantine Studies, 1986.

The Chronicle of Theophanes Confessor: Byzantine and Near Eastern History AD 284–813. Translated with introduction and commentary by Cyril Mango and Roger Scott. Oxford: Clarendon Press, 1997.

Clavijo, Ruy Gonzales de. *Narrative of the Embassy to the Court of Timour at Samarkand, A.D. 1403–6*. Translated by Clements R. Markham. New York: Burt Franklin Publisher, 1970. First printed in 1859 for the Hakluyt Society in London.

The Itinerary of Benjamin of Tudela. Critical text, translation and commentary by Marcus Nathan Adler. London: Oxford University Press, 1907.

Komnena, Anna. *Anne Comnene: Alexiade*, three vols. Edited and translated by Bernard Leib. Paris: Bude, 1937–45.

Mango, Cyril. *The Art of the Byzantine Empire, 312–1453: Sources and Documents*. Toronto: Toronto University Press, 1986.

Nasûhü's Silâhi. *Beyan-ı Menâzil-i Sefer-i Irâkeyn-i Sultân Süleymân Hân* (Istanbul: Rare Masterpieces Department of Istanbul University Library), T 5964.

O City of Byzantium: Annals of Niketas Choniates. Translated by Harry J. Magoulias. Detroit, MI: Wayne State University Press, 1984.

Porphyrogennetos, Constantine. *The Book of Ceremonies*, two vols. Translated by Anne Moffatt and Maxeme Tall. Canberra: Australian Association for Byzantine Studies, 2012.

Procopius. *The Secret History: With Related Texts*. Translated and edited with an introduction by Anthony Kaldellis. Indianapolis: Hackett Publishing, 2010.

St. John Chrysostom. *On Wealth and Poverty*. Translated by Catharine P. Roth. Crestwood, NY: St Vladimir's Seminary Press, 1984.

Secondary Sources

Akyürek, Engin. 'Konstantinopolis Hipodromu'. In *Türk ve İslam Eserleri Müzesi: 100 Yıl Önce 100 Yıl Sonra*, edited by Seracettin Şahin,

Sevgi Kutluay, and Miyase Çelen, 144 9. Ankara: T. C. Kültür ve Turizm Bakanlığı Yayınları, 2014.

Atasoy, Nurhan. *Surname-i Humayun: An Imperial Celebration*. Istanbul: Koçbank Yayınları, 1997.

Atasoy, Nurhan. *Silahşor, Tarihçi, Matematikçi, Nakkaş, Hattat: Matrakçı Nasuh ve Menzilnamesi*. Istanbul: Masa, 2015.

Bardill, Jonathan. 'Hippodrom'da Kazılar ve Arkeologlar/Archaeologists and Excavations in the Hippodrome'. In *Hippodrom/Atmeydanı: İstanbul'un Tarih Sahnesi/Hippodrome/Atmeydanı: A Stage for Istanbul's History*, vol. 1, edited by Brigitte Pitarakis, 83–90. Istanbul: Pera Müzesi Yayınları, 2010.

Bardill, Jonathan. 'Konstantinopolis Hippodromu'nun Anıtları ve Süslemeleri/ The Monuments and Decoration of the Hippodrome in Constantinople'. In *Hippodrom/Atmeydanı: İstanbul'un Tarih Sahnesi/Hippodrome/Atmeydanı: A Stage for Istanbul's History*, vol. 1, edited by Brigitte Pitarakis, 149–84. Istanbul: Pera Müzesi Yayınları, 2010.

Bardill, Jonathan. 'Konstantinopolis Hippodromu'nun Mimarisi ve Arkeolojisi/ The Architecture and Archaeology of the Hippodrome in Constantinople'. In *Hippodrom/Atmeydanı: İstanbul'un Tarih Sahnesi/Hippodrome/Atmeydanı: A Stage for Istanbul's History*, vol. 1, edited by Brigitte Pitarakis, 91–148. Istanbul: Pera Müzesi Yayınları, 2010.

Bassett, Sarah G. 'The Antiquities in the Hippodrome of Constantinople'. *Dumbarton Oaks Papers* 45 (1991): 87–96.

Cameron, Alan. *Porphyrius the Charioteer*. New York: Oxford University Press, 1973.

Cameron, Alan. *Circus Factions, Blues and Greens at Rome and Byzantium*. Oxford: Clarendon Press, 1976.

Cameron, Averil. *The Mediterranean World in Late Antiquity, A.D. 395–400*. London and New York: Routledge, 1993.

Casson, Stanley, David Talbot Rice, A. Hugh Martin Jones, and Geoffrey Francis Hudson. *Preliminary Report upon the Excavations Carried Out in the Hippodrome of Constantinople in 1927 on Behalf of the British Academy*. London: Oxford University Press, 1928.

Casson, Stanley, David Talbot Rice, Basil Gray, and Geoffrey Francis Hudson. *Second Report upon the Excavations Carried Out in and Near the Hippodrome of Constantinople in 1928 on Behalf of the British Academy*. London: Oxford University Press, 1929.

Dagron, Gilbert. 'Bir Roma'dan Diğerine/From One Rome to the Other'. In *Hippodrom/Atmeydanı: İstanbul'un Tarih Sahnesi/Hippodrome/Atmeydanı: A Stage for Istanbul's History*, vol. 1, edited by Brigitte Pitarakis, 29–35. Istanbul: Pera Müzesi Yayınları, 2010.

Dagron, Gilbert. *L'hippodrome de Constantinople: Jeux, peuple et politique.* Bibliothèque des Histoires. Paris: Éditions Gallimard, 2011.

Demangel, Robert, and Ernest Mamboury. *Le Quartier des Manganes et la première région de Constantinople.* Recherches françaises en Turquie 2. Paris: Éditions de Boccard, 1939.

Diehl, Charles. 'The Byzantine Civilization'. In *The Cambridge Medieval History, Vol. 4: The Eastern Roman Empire (717–1453),* edited by Joseph R. Tanner, Charles W. Previté-Orton, and Zachary N. Brooke, 745–77. Cambridge: Cambridge University Press, 1927.

Duyuran, Rüstem. 'İstanbul Adalet Sarayı inşaatı yerinde yapılan kazılar hakkındaki ilk rapor/First Report on Excavations on the Site of the New Palace of Justice at Istanbul'. *İstanbul Arkeoloji Müzeleri Yıllığı* 5 (1952): 23–32, 33–8.

Duyuran, Rüstem. 'İstanbul Adalet Sarayı inşaat yerinde yapılan kazılar hakkında ikinci rapor/Second Report on Excavations on the Site of the New Palace of Justice at Istanbul'. *İstanbul Arkeoloji Müzeleri Yıllığı* 6 (1953): 21–7, 74–80.

Evans, James Allan. *The Emperor Justinian and the Byzantine Empire.* Greenwood Guides to Historic Events of the Ancient World. Westport, CT and London: Greenwood Press, 2005.

Geanakoplos, Deno John. *Byzantium: Church, Society, and Civilization Seen through Contemporary Eyes.* Chicago: University of Chicago Press, 1984.

Guilland, Rodolphe. 'The Hippodrome at Byzantium'. *Speculum* 23, no. 4 (1948): 676–82.

Humphrey, John H. *Roman Circuses: Arenas for Chariot Racing.* London: Batsford, 1986.

Kaegi, Walter Emil, and Alexander Kazhdan, 'Tribonian'. In *The Oxford Dictionary of Byzantium,* edited by Alexander Kahzdan, Alice-Mary Talbot, Anthony Cutler, Timothy E. Gregory, and Nancy Petterson Ševčenko, 2114. New York and Oxford: Oxford University Press, 1991.

Liddell, Henry George, Robert Scott, Henery Stuart Jones, and Roderick McKenzie. *A Greek and English Lexicon.* Oxford: Clarendon Press, 1940.

Majesca, George P. *Russian Travelers to Constantinople in the Fourteenth and Fifteenth Centuries.* Washington, DC: Dumbarton Oaks, 1984.

Mango, Cyril. 'Konstantinopolis Hippodromu'nun Tarihçesi/A History of the Hippodrome of Constantinople'. In *Hippodrom/Atmeydanı: İstanbul'un Tarih Sahnesi/Hippodrome/Atmeydanı: A Stage for Istanbul's History,* vol. 1, edited by Brigitte Pitarakis, 36–43. Istanbul: Pera Müzesi Yayınları, 2010.

Mango, Cyril, Alexander Kazhdan, and Anthony Cutler, 'Hippodromes'. In *The Oxford Dictionary of Byzantium*, edited by Alexander Kahzdan, Alice-Mary Talbot, Anthony Cutler, Timothy E. Gregory, and Nancy Petterson Ševčenko 934–6. New York and Oxford: Oxford University Press, 1991.

Ménage, Victor Louis. 'The Serpent Column in Ottoman Sources'. *Anatolian Studies* 14 (1964): 169–73.

Müller-Wiener, Wolfgang. *Bildlexikon zur Topographi Istanbuls: Byzantion, Konstantinupolis, Istanbul bis zum Beginn des 17 Jahrhunderts*. Tübingen: Ernst Wasmuth Verlag, 1977.

Naumann, Rudolf, and Hans Belting. *Die Euphemia-Kirche am Hippodrom zu Istanbul und ihre Fresken*. Istanbuler Forschungen 25. Berlin: Verlag Gebr. Mann, 1966.

Pitarakis, Brigitte, ed. *Hippodrom/Atmeydanı: İstanbul'un Tarih Sahnesi/ Hippodrome/Atmeydanı: A Stage for Istanbul's History*, vol. 1. Istanbul: Pera Müzesi Yayınları, 2010.

Roueché, Charlotte. 'Partiler ve Eğlenceler/The Factions and Entertainment'. In *Hippodrom/Atmeydanı: İstanbul'un Tarih Sahnesi/Hippodrome/Atmeydanı: A Stage for Istanbul's History*, vol. 1, edited by Brigitte Pitarakis, 50–63. Istanbul: Pera Müzesi Yayınları, 2010.

Strootman, Rolf. 'The Serpent Column: The Persistent Meanings of a Pagan Relic in Christian and Islamic Constantinople'. *Material Religion* 10, no. 4 (2014): 432–51.

Talbot, Alice-Mary. 'Orta Bizans Döneminde Hippodrom'un Cazibesi/The Lure of the Hippodrome in the Middle Byzantine Era'. In *Hippodrom/ Atmeydanı: İstanbul'un Tarih Sahnesi/Hippodrome/Atmeydanı: A Stage for Istanbul's History*, vol. 1, edited by Brigitte Pitarakis, 65–8. Istanbul: Pera Müzesi Yayınları, 2010.

Treadgold, Warren. *A History of the Byzantine State and Society*. Stanford, CA: Stanford University Press, 1997.

Vasiliev, Aleksandr A. 'The Monument of Porphyrius in the Hippodrome at Constantinople'. *Dumbarton Oaks Papers* 4 (1948): 27–49.

Yazıcı, Nurcan. 'İlk Osmanlı Sergi Binası ve Mimar Bourgeois – Parvillée – Montani İşbirliği/The First Ottoman Exhibition Building in Atmeydanı and the Collaboration of Architects Bourgeois – Parvillée – Montani'. In *Hippodrom/Atmeydanı: İstanbul'un Tarih Sahnesi/Hippodrome/Atmeydanı: A Stage for Istanbul's History*, vol. 2, edited by Ekrem Işın, 128–51. Istanbul: Pera Müzesi Yayınları, 2010.

Cambridge Elements ᵉ

The History of Constantinople

Peter Frankopan
University of Oxford

Peter Frankopan is Professor of Global History at Oxford University, where he is also Director of the Centre for Byzantine Research and Senior Research Fellow at Worcester College. He specialises in the history of the Eastern Mediterranean from antiquity to the modern day, and is the author of the best-sellers *The Silk Roads: A New History of the World* (2015) and *The New Silk Roads: The Future and Present of the World* (2018).

About the Series
Telling the history of Constantinople through its monuments and people, leading scholars present a rich and unbiased account of this ever-evolving metropolis. From its foundation to the domination of the Ottoman Empire to contemporary Istanbul, numerous aspects of Constantinople's narrative are explored in this unrivalled series.

Cambridge Elements ᵔ

The History of Constantinople

Printed in the United States
by Baker & Taylor Publisher Services